Handbook of Chemical Warfare and Terrorism

Handbook of Chemical Warfare and Terrorism

STEVEN L. HOENIG

GREENWOOD PRESS
Westport, Connecticut • London

Library of Congress Cataloging-in-Publication Data

Hoenig, Steven L., 1957–
Handbook of chemical warfare and terrorism / Steven L. Hoenig.
p. cm.
Includes bibliographical references and index.
ISBN 0–313–32407–7 (alk. paper)
1. Chemical warfare—Handbooks, manuals, etc. 2. Chemical agents (Munitions)—Handbooks, manuals, etc. 3. Chemical terrorism—Handbooks, manuals, etc. I. Title.
UG447.H62 2002
358'.34—dc21 2002067841

British Library Cataloguing in Publication Data is available.

Library of Congress Catalog Card Number: 2002067841
ISBN: 0–313–32407–7

First published in 2002

Greenwood Press, 88 Post Road West, Westport, CT 06881
An imprint of Greenwood Publishing Group, Inc.
www.greenwood.com

Printed in the United States of America

The paper used in this book complies with the Permanent Paper Standard issued by the National Information Standards Organization (Z39.48–1984).

10 9 8 7 6 5 4 3 2 1

For Lena

Contents

Preface

In recent years, especially since the 11 September 2001 terrorist attacks, the Gulf War, and the Japanese subway terrorist attack, the subject of chemical warfare has become commonplace. Numerous material has been written on the subject, most dealing with the subject at various points in history, its suspected use, the casualties from its use, the ethics of using chemical agents, and the politics surrounding the subject.

This book addresses the technical side of the subject. There is relatively little material easily available to the public regarding the scientific aspects. The majority of the material that is available has been written for the military by the military or by hazardous material (Hazmat) personnel.

Hopefully, this book gives the reader, in one handy source, a variety of material needed to understand what chemical warfare agents exist, how they can be delivered, how to protect against them, how to decontaminate them, and how to detect them.

The first chapter is meant to introduce the reader to the concept of chemical warfare. It covers a brief history of chemical warfare as well as the what other nations possess chemical warfare capabilities and those likely to. It also defines a chemical warfare agent is and the various classes into which they fall. A section also covers how various onditions affect the ability of chemical warfare agents to contaminate a given area and how they act in given circumstances. There is also a section of the terminology that is used throughout the second chapter.

Chapter 2 lists the different classes of chemical warfare agents. They fall into several categories — blister, blood, choking, incapacitating, nerve, tear, and vomit agents. Chemical agents have traditionally fallen into one of these categories. Also listed in this chapter are some the more important chemical and physical properties that chemical agents possess.

The third chapter covers the current U.S. chemical weapons delivery systems. Although currently the U.S. stockpile of chemical weapons is in the process of being destroyed, it is still relevant to be aware of the capabilities that the United States possesses. As can be seen from this chapter, the construction of a delivery system is not overly difficult, and the capability of another country can be extrapolated from that of the United States.

Chapter 4 covers the subject of protection and decontamination against chemical agents. The chapter covers civilian and military capabilities, on and off the battlefield. The U.S. military capabilities in the area of chemical warfare are rather extensive and quite detailed. This is not unexpected since the military, particularly the U.S. Army, has been extensively involved in chemical warfare since its inception. Any organization that is in need of information should first look to the military. Many of the procedures, concepts, and material utilized by the military can be easily adopted for civilian use.

Chapter 5 has a rather extensive list of equipment and the capabilities of the various items listed. The equipment falls into several categories, such as detection, decontamination, individual and collective protection, and medical treatment for chemical agents.

The Appendix is a list of abbreviations and acronyms that are used throughout this book and many other manuals that cover this subject.

Acknowledgments

I wish to express my deepest graditude to Richard Kolodkin for his assistance and friendship.

I also wish to thank Lieutenant Colonel William J. Vorlicek, Assistant Chief of Staff, 53rd Troop Command, New York Army National Guard for his expertise and his extensive knowledge in the field of nuclear, biological, and chemical (NBC) warfare, as well as his careful scrutiny of the manuscript.

Once again, I extend my deep gratitude to Richard Leff, without whose help I would not be here to write this book.

1

Introduction

CHEMICAL WEAPONS

A U.S. government agency has noted that, "unlike nuclear weapons, which require a large, specialized, and costly scientific-industrial base, chemical agents can be made with commercial equipment generally available to any country. Indeed, few military technologies have evolved as little as chemical weapons over the past half century."

Over the last few years the use or threat of their use has sharply increased. From the stockpiles of chemical weapons in Iraq, to their reported use in the Kosovo crisis, chemical weapons have taken the spotlight. The U.S. government recognized that chemical weapons were becoming more prevalent than ever before and that defensive steps were needed. In 1994 Congress passed Public Law #103-160, which mandates that the secretary of defense shall submit an annual report on chemical and biological warfare defense programs. It was determined that the combat readiness of the armed forces was deficient in chemical defense, and in recent years not only has the budget for chemical defense research increased, but a sharp increase in the training of military forces in the areas of chemical defense has occurred.

Effects

Chemical weapons use lethal gases or liquids that attack either the body's nervous system, blood, skin, or lungs. They are capable of producing effects such as tearing, blistering, vomiting, hallucinations, or loss of nervous control.

Chemical attacks can contaminate an area from between several hours to several days, contaminating equipment and forcing troops to wear highly restrictive and physically demanding protective clothing, thereby reducing their combat efficiency. Additionally, chemical weapons may compromise the operational effectiveness of military forces by requiring collective protective measures and decontamination which would strain the logistics of human and physical resources.

Chemical attacks can cause widespread panic among both the military and civilian populations, and their terror effects on civilians are potent. The large number of potential casualties would place excessive burdens on local and military resources.

The intimidatory nature of chemical weapons is such that a chemical attack or the threat of such an attack could cause wholesale disruption or breakdown of civil and economic activity in the affected area. The psychological effect on a civilian population is likely to cause panic or terror.

Methods of Delivery

Chemical weapons can be delivered by a wide variety of weapon systems, including missiles, aerial bombs, artillery shells, and land mines. According to a General Accounting Office report, during the Iran–Iraq War, Iraq delivered mustard gas and tabun with artillery shells, aerial bombs, missiles, rockets, grenades, and bursting smoke munitions. The Soviets have Scud-B and FROG-7 weapons, which can deliver warheads filled with a chemical agent, Iraq also has chemical warheads on its modified Scud missiles but did not use them during the Gulf War, and North Korea is also believed to have developed chemical warheads for its Scud-B and Scud-C ballistic missiles.

However, chemical agent-filled warheads delivered by ballistic missiles pose some complex engineering problems. Each warhead would have to be engineered to a specific agent since each agent has different and unique properties. For maximum effectiveness the warheads are fused to detonate at a set altitude depending on the agent carried, and different agents require different concentrations and dispersals in order to be effective. For this reason, missiles fitted with spray tanks would serve as particularly effective delivery vehicles.

Limitations

Chemical weapons, more than most other armaments, depend upon atmospheric and topographical factors. Temperature, weather conditions, and terrain are important factors in determining the persistence of a given chemical agent. Large quantities of agents may be required to achieve high lethality, and some chemical agents degrade rapidly, allowing areas, buildings, and equipment affected to be reused (even if they require decontamination first). An attacker's use of persistent agents may mean that areas that an attacker wishes to move across or occupy remain contaminated, necessitating the use of protective equipment and/or decontamination for the attacking force. Warning devices against chemical attack tend to be more accurate and sensitive than those against biological attack.

In certain circumstances, the military strategy of chemical attacks is not significantly greater than that of conventional strikes and offers few war-fighting advantages. As noted, however, the most potent effects of chemical weapons are psychological and intimidatory.

Potential Targets

The potential targets of chemical weapons include troop concentrations, dispersal areas, logistics centers, command and control centers, air bases, ports, key infrastructure installations (oil and power facilities, desalination plants, etc.), and civilian population centers.

We need to explore the role of chemical weapons not only in conflicts involving organized military establishments but also as a potential weapon for terrorist use.

The impact of a terrorist attack using chemical weapons can be as great as or even greater, under the right set of circumstances than, any terrorist attack using conventional weapons. For instance, the Oklahoma City bombing killed 168 people and wounded hundreds, the 1993 World Trade Center bombing killed 6 and wounded over 1,000, and the attack on the USS *Cole* killed 17 and wounded 38. The sarin attack by the Aum Shinrikyo cult group in a Japanese subway killed 12 and wounded over 5,500. The significant difference between the bombings and the nerve agent attack is that in the bombings, hundreds of pounds of explosives were used, whereas in the nerve agent attack only a few pounds of agent were used. Even more significant is the fact that it was done by wrapping the agent in a small package and leaving it on a subway car.

BRIEF HISTORY OF CHEMICAL AGENTS

At the beginning of the twentieth century the Germans were leaders in industrial chemistry, and so when World War I broke out, it was only natural that they applied their chemical expertise to warfare as well. For all practical purposes this can be considered the birth of chemical warfare.

1914–1915

The birth of chemical warfare can be traced largely back to a single man: chemist Fritz Haber, who developed poison gases for Germany during World War I. He was a world-famous chemist who had developed a crucial process for extracting nitrates from the atmosphere. This process was used to manufacture fertilizer and later to make explosives.

When the war broke out in August 1914, Germany was confident of victory, but soon its offensive bogged down in a stalemate of trench warfare in the West. With the war front deadlocked, Haber focused on what he could contribute to a German victory. He believed that poison gas would be able to penetrate trenches and fortifications, allowing the German army to achieve major breakthroughs through Allied defenses.

Poison gases of various sorts were already available as unwanted by-products of chemical processes. At his Berlin institute, founded by the kaiser himself, Haber began experimenting with, and refining, such gases to find one suitable for battlefield use. He focused on chlorine gas, which was used in the dye industry.

At the end of 1914 Haber approached the German military to persuade them to use poison gas, but the military had no great respect for scientists, and poison gases seemed unsporting to many military men. Haber was able to convince them to watch a demonstration, which was conducted at a military testing ground outside Cologne.

With the stalemate on the front continuing, the German military were no longer confident of victory. Defeat would be the greatest dishonor, so in early 1915 they decided to swallow their scruples and use Haber's chemical weapons. They gave him officer's rank, and he helped organize a chemical corps.

The first chlorine gas attack occurred on 22 April 1915 against French and Algerian troops facing them at Ypres in Belgium, as 5,730 cylinders of chlorine gas were set up and the valves opened to create a cloud blowing over the ground toward the enemy. The 180 tons of gas released formed a dense, green cloud that rolled into Allied lines.

With 30 parts of chlorine to 1 million parts of air, chlorine gas is a nasty irritant that causes harsh coughing. At 1,000 parts per million, it is lethal, caustically stripping the lining from the lungs and causing victims to drown in their own fluids.

The results of the gas attack were devastating. The French and Algerians choked, their lungs burned, and they slowly died. The gas cloud tinted everything a sickly green. Those who could escape the cloud fled in panic. Before dawn on 24 April 1915, the Germans poured gas into Canadian lines, with similar results.

Allied casualties in the two days of attacks were estimated at 5,000 dead and 10,000 disabled, half of them permanently. Despite the fact that the French had captured a German soldier who was carrying a gas mask and who under interrogation provided advance details of the attack, the report was lost, and the soldiers in the trenches had no warning.

The attack was unbelievably effective. Irritant chemicals, essentially tear gases, had already been fired in artillery shells by both the French and the Germans, but they had not proven to be much more than a tactical annoyance. Even the German military were astonished by the results of Haber's chlorine gas, but to Haber's fury they were not prepared to exploit the breach that they had made in Allied lines.

The Germans launched a number of gas attacks during May 1915, with the last attack taking place on 24 May 1915. The prevailing winds over the front lines had changed direction, and except for two small-scale attacks in October 1915, the Germans did not return to gas attacks on the Western Front until December.

The change in prevailing winds did allow the Germans to turn their attention to the Russians on the Eastern Front. On 31 May 1915, Haber supervised the first chlorine gas attack on the Eastern Front. Gas proved extremely deadly against the poorly equipped Russians, though it was not very effective during the cold winters, as it tended to freeze.

1915–1916

In response to the German use of poison gases, the British army assigned Major Charles Howard Foulkes of the Royal Engineers to devise a response to the gas attacks.

In June 1915, 2.5 million "Hypo Helmets" were issued to Allied troops. These were crude gas masks, made of flannel, with eyepieces made out of celluloid and chemically impregnated to neutralize chlorine. They were better than nothing, but they could not resist an extended gas attack.

By early fall, Foulkes and his "Special Companies," later Special Brigades, were ready to respond to German gas attacks with one of their own. On 25 September 1915, the British conducted their first gas attack at Loos, Belgium, using 5,500 cylinders of chlorine gas, in support of a major ground offensive.

The gas attack had mixed results. At one point the gas blew back into Allied lines, resulting in thousands of Allied casualties. However, the effect of gas on the Germans was brutal, and the Allies were able to quickly overrun the Germans' front line trenches. It did little good. The British soon found themselves against the German rear defenses and suffered 50,000 casualties at Loos. The Germans counterattacked and pushed back the penetrations within a week.

On 9 December 1915, with the winds again in their favor, the Germans launched another gas attack on the Allied lines, this time against the British at Ypres in Belgium. The Germans used chlorine and introduced a new agent, phosgene.

Phosgene was another industrial chemical by-product that Fritz Haber and his institute had evaluated as a weapon. Its lethal concentration was only 1/18th that of chlorine, and its action was delayed. A lethal dose of phosgene would cause some irritation at first and then pass for a day or two. In many cases, men would simply shrug off the gas attack as inconsequential or hardly notice that they had been gassed. Then the linings of their lungs would break down, and as with chlorine gas, they would drown in their own lung fluids, coughing up a watery stream until they choked and died.

Fortunately, the British had realized the summer before that phosgene might be used as a chemical weapon and were prepared for it. They had developed the improved "P Helmet," with better impregnation for protection against gas and a rubber exhaust tube. Nine million P Helmets had been issued by December and managed to limit Allied casualties.

The British were quick to adopt phosgene in response. In June 1916, during the Battle of the Somme, they used the new gas, pouring out a huge cloud of phosgene and chlorine gas along a 27-kilometer (17-mile) front. The cloud penetrated up to 19 kilometers (12 miles) behind German lines, killing everything unprotected. The British became particularly fond of phosgene.

In 1915, both sides had only been experimenting with poison gas, but by 1916 it became a standard weapon and was used in great quantity. The British established a large research and development facility on Salisbury Plain at a place named Porton Down for development of chemical weapons.

However, the Allies were at a significant disadvantage in chemical warfare. Germany's chemical industry was the biggest in the world. Germany's eight giant chemical firms were united in a cartel named the Interessen Gemeinschaft (IG). The IG was willing and capable of producing large quantities of chemical weapons.

Soldiers hated poison gas more than they hated the conventional weapons used against them. Trench war was bad enough; gas made it much more dreadful. Soldiers were just as scared of their own gas as they were of the enemy's, since accidents in handling gas weapons were common, and changes in wind direction made the gas releases potentially dangerous to everyone. During the Battle of the Somme, 57 of Foulkes' men were killed by their own gas. Gas masks were extremely uncomfortable, and the terror caused by a gas attack was extreme, particularly after the introduction of phosgene.

1916–1918

The technology for gas warfare continued to improve. In early 1916, both the French and the Germans started firing gas shells out of conventional artillery, and the British began to use gas barrages on a large scale the next year. Artillery shells could not achieve the gas concentrations available with cylinders, but they could reach far into enemy lines and so were less dependent on the wind.

While the Allies at first lagged behind the Germans in developing new gas weapons, they soon came up with innovations of their own. The first was the British Livens Projector, invented by British army officer Captain F. H. Livens.

The Livens Projector was simply a metal pipe approximately a meter long that was buried in the soil at a 45-degree angle. Each projector was loaded with a drum containing about 14 kilograms (30 pounds) of gas; the projector was then fired by an electrical charge, sending the drums tumbling through air for a range of over a kilometer and a half (about a mile).

Each drum contained a bursting charge to blast it open when it landed near enemy trenches, dousing the enemy with gas with little warning. The Livens Projector was cheap, crude, and extremely effective, as it could be used in mass numbers to produce an overwhelming and terrifying barrage. It was first used at the Battle of Arras on 9 April 1917. As a witness observed:

> The discharge took place practically simultaneously: a dull red flash seemed to flicker all along the front as far as the eye could reach, and there was a slight ground tremor, followed a little later by a muffled roar, as 2,340 of these sinister projectiles hurtled through space, turning clumsily over and over, and some of them, no doubt, colliding in flight.
>
> About 20 seconds later they landed in masses in the German positions, and after a brief pause the steel cases were burst open by the explosive charges inside, and nearly fifty tons of liquid phosgene were liberated which vaporized instantly and formed a cloud that Livens, who watched the discharge from an aeroplane, noticed it still so thick as to be visible as it floated over Vimy and Bailleu villages.

The British became very proficient at setting up and using massed Livens Projectors and developed a range of projectiles for them. The Germans tried to copy the projector, but it gave the British an edge on the Germans in chemical warfare.

The Germans had a trick of their own, however. On the evening of 12 July 1917, the Germans fired shells into British trenches at Ypres, but when they burst, the shells released a brown, oily fluid, not a gas. The stuff smelled horrible, something like rotten garlic or mustard, but it otherwise didn't seem particularly offensive and caused only slight irritation to eyes and throat.

Remarkably, given the paranoia over gas attacks, many British troops didn't bother to put on gas masks. As the night wore on, they began to feel increasing pain in their eyes and throat and gradually began to suffer swelling and huge blisters wherever their skin had come into contact with the noxious fluid.

The Germans called their new weapon "Lost," or "Yellow Cross" after the marking on shells, in contrast to the "Green Cross" that designated chlorine and phosgene. The French quickly named it "Yperite," after its use at Ypres. The British code-named it "HS," for "Hun Stuff," but gave it another name that stuck: mustard gas.

Its formal name was dichloroethyl sulfide. It was a blistering agent, or "vesicant" in formal medical terms, and had actually been evaluated by the British sometime earlier and rejected for not being lethal enough. Although mustard gas didn't have the killing power of phosgene as such, that didn't make it any less useful as a weapon. The Germans had realized that improved gas masks and training had neutralized the military usefulness of phosgene against the British and French. Fritz Haber then put his skills to work to develop a gas for which a gas mask could offer no protection.

Mustard gas did not dissipate like the other gases. The oily fluid could persist for a long time and continue to cause misery and pain to anyone who came in contact with it, accidentally getting some of it on his boots and from there on his hands and then on his face. It would freeze over the winter and still prove dangerous when it thawed again in the spring.

Manufacturing mustard gas was difficult and dangerous. The French were not able to begin full production until June 1918. The British built a large plant at Avonmouth to manufacture mustard gas.

Not until September 1918 did the British army obtain mustard gas, and the Allies never seriously used mustard gas in combat. The British made do with what they had with a vengeance. In early 1918, the British responded to the German mustard gas attacks with dense clouds of phosgene, released from big cylinders on train cars moved up behind the lines.

The Germans launched their last major offensive in the West in March 1918. After winning major successes at first, the offensive fizzled out, and the Allies, now including massive American reinforcements, pushed back the Germans relentlessly.

Gas could be highly effective if used against opponents not equipped to deal with it. As mentioned, the Germans used it with great effect against the Russians, inflicting what is now estimated to be a half million casualties, and in October 1917, the Germans used phosgene to break the Italian defense line in northern Italy at Caporetto. The unprepared Italians were sent into terrified flight and decisively defeated.

Troops equipped and trained to deal with gas attacks suffered relatively minimal casualties, though bundling up against gas was stifling and exhausting, and life in a poisoned landscape was demoralizing.

One incident in particular should be noted. On 14 October 1918, the British fired their new mustard gas shells into German positions at a Belgian village named Werwick. One of the injured was a corporal named Adolf Hitler. He was evacuated back to Germany by train a few days later, blinded and burned.

In November 1918 an armistice was declared, and the shooting stopped. Gas was estimated to have killed about 100,000 men and injured 1 million. The number of men killed by gas was small compared to the number killed by other means, but gas had played a particularly unpleasant role in the conflict.

1918–1934

Fearing that he would be tried as a war criminal, Fritz Haber left Germany for Switzerland wearing a fake beard. He needn't have worried, in 1919 he was awarded the Nobel Prize in chemistry for his prewar development of the Haber process and was restored to respectability, though there were loud protests at the award. Haber himself hardly seemed contrite and did not avoid the subject of gas warfare when he received the prize, saying: "In no future war will the military be able to ignore poison gas. It is a higher form of killing."

The military were hardly ignoring it. Three classes of gas agents has been introduced in the war:

- Asphyxiants such as chlorine and phosgene, which attacked the lungs.
- Blistering agents, consisting of several different forms of mustard gas. The original German chemical agent was sulfur mustard, but various nitrogen mustard agents were synthesized and manufactured as well.
- Blood agents, most specifically, hydrogen cyanide (HCN), also known as prussic acid, which blocked the absorption of oxygen in the blood. Cyanides had been used in combat by the Allies to an extent, but though deadly in enclosed spaces, they tended to dissipate quickly in open air and had little useful effect at low concentrations.

Gas shells and other delivery systems had been refined, as had been defensive technologies and procedures. All the combatants had been preparing even nastier chemical weapons when the war ended. The Germans had invented an improved projector named the Gaswerfer. The Americans, new to the chemical warfare game, invented a blistering agent named lewisite that was similar to mustard gas in its ability to cause damage to a victim's entire body but acted much faster, causing immediate agony in an unprotected environment.

Fritz Haber continued his work on poison gases under the cover of "pest control," as chemical weapons had been forbidden to the Germans by the Treaty of Versailles in 1919. He developed an insecticide that could be used to fumigate buildings. It could also be deadly to humans in an enclosed space. It was known as Zyklon B, and the Nazis would find it a useful substance for their extermination camps 20 years later.

Some sketchy reports indicated that gas warfare continued in the years immediately after World War I, if on a very small and quiet scale. Gas shells were apparently used in the Russian civil war by both the White and Red Armies. The British were believed to have used chemical weapons on hill tribesmen in Afghanistan, and other colonial powers were thought to have found gas a useful weapon to help suppress rebellious populations.

If chemical warfare continued in secret, in public it was made illegal through a series of international treaties that culminated in the Geneva Protocol of 1925. Thirty-eight countries signed the protocol, renouncing the use of chemical weapons, though the treaty was not ratified by the United States and Japan.

There were major loopholes in the treaty; it had few or no verification or enforcement clauses, and the major powers continued to develop chemical weapons in secret. During the late 1920s, the Soviets began to develop their own chemical warfare capability with cooperation from Weimar Germany, and in the same time frame the Japanese began their own chemical warfare capability.

The Japanese proved industrious in their chemical weapons efforts, producing mustard gas and lewisite; chemical bombs, rockets, aerial dispensers, antitank grenades using hydrogen cyanide charges, and other weapons; and chemical protective gear not only for men but for horses, camels, and dogs.

When the Nazis came to power in Germany in 1933, they were very interested in chemical warfare. Hitler had been impressed by its capabilities after his incapacitation after a gas attack, and in the form of Fritz Haber, Germany possessed a great resource for chemical warfare. However, Haber's Jewish background made him distasteful to the Nazis. His stature was such that he was told that he could remain in charge of his research but that all his Jewish workers must resign. He replied that he would resign as well. He left Germany and died in Switzerland the next year, in 1934.

1934–1940

Gas warfare continued to evolve without Fritz Haber. Another German chemist, Gerhard Schrader developed a highly lethal organophosphate compound in December 1936, which he named tabun. He found out how potentially lethal it was in January 1937, when he and an assistant accidentally spilled a drop of it. Their pupils constricted to pinholes, and they suffered shortness of breath. Had the dose been slightly greater, it would have killed them.

Tabun was the first member of a fourth class of poison gases, known as "nerve gases." It was discovered a few years later that it worked by interfering with the transmission of nerve impulses across synapses. Victims lose control of their body until they can no longer breathe, causing suffocation. The gas was invisible and odorless and could kill in extremely tiny quantities. Since nerve agents can be absorbed through the skin, a gas mask is of little protection.

Tabun was far too dangerous to be used safely as a pesticide. However, Schrader realized the military potential of his discovery and reported his discovery to the authorities, as was required under Nazi law of any discovery that might have military applications. Unlike Haber, Schrader was not enthusiastic about developing chemical weapons, but he did it nonetheless. The Nazis set him up in a secret military research lab. In 1938, he discovered an even more lethal nerve gas similar to tabun, which he named sarin.

When war broke out in September 1939, tabun wasn't available for operational use, but the Germans had a chemical corps that conducted field exercises using mustard gas. However, the Germans did not use gases during their offensives. Gas was basically a siege weapon, intended to attack troops dug into trenches and fortifications, and the German blitzkrieg was war of rapid mobility. Gas could hamper the attacker as much as hurt the defender.

The Germans stockpiled chemical agents anyway. In January 1940, the Germans began high-priority construction of a huge tabun plant at Dyenfurtham-Oder in Silesia, now part of Poland. The plant was to perform all phases of tabun production, though a long series of production glitches kept the plant out of operation until April 1942.

Producing tabun was no simple task. Some of the intermediate chemicals were extremely corrosive and required vessels lined with silver or quartz. The final product was so incredibly toxic that final production was in rooms with double glass walls through which pressurized air circulated.

The units had to be decontaminated periodically and then with steam and ammonia. The workers had to wear rubberized clothes with respirators, and the suits were disposed of after their 10th use. If a worker was contaminated, his protective clothes were quickly stripped off, and he was dunked in a sodium bicarbonate bath.

A number of accidents at the Dyenfurth plant killed at least 10 workers. One had two liters of tabun poured down the neck of his suit. He lived for two minutes, despite all attempts to save his life.

In the meantime, chemical warfare had returned to the public eye again. The Italians used mustard gas during their campaign in Abyssinia (now Ethiopia) in 1937. They added the new feature of dropping it from airplanes in aerial bombs. World opinion soon condemned Mussolini.

Beginning in 1937, the Japanese also began to use chemical weapons against the Chinese. China was remote and not of as much concern as Europe, and so information on the Japanese use of chemical warfare was sketchy, but reports trickled out of mustard gas attacks on Chinese soldiers and citizens.

Chemical warfare was coming back into style. With war fears in Europe rising, European governments began to prepare for chemical warfare. The British distributed 30 million gas masks, not knowing how useless they would be if the Germans used their new secret nerve gas tabun, and implemented an exhaustive chemical civil defense program. Governments also ramped up development and production of chemical weapons.

The experience of World War I gave most of the nations entering World War II the expectation that chemical weapons would be used to an even greater extent. Newspaper articles and popular fiction predicted that chemical weapons would turn entire regions of Europe into lifeless wastelands.

To almost everyone's surprise, it didn't happen. A fragile stalemate kept chemical weapons out of action during World War II. The use of chemical weapons also remained restrained in the postwar period, though the balance between attempts at control and the pressure toward their use became increasingly unstable.

1940–1945

As the war turned against Nazi Germany, and Allied bombers pounded German cities to rubble, the incentive to use chemical weapons rose. By 1944, the Nazis had enough tabun to kill everyone in London, as well as large stockpiles of a wide range of more traditional chemical agents.

They were not used, not even at the Allied invasion at Normandy, when Allied forces were almost completely defenseless against gas attack. This appears to be partly due to the fact that Hitler had been gassed himself, but more likely, there was a peculiar complementary misunderstanding between the two sides.

British intelligence proved much more competent in World War II than German intelligence, but German security concerning nerve agents was very tight, and the Allies did not know that such weapons existed. On the other hand, German researchers knew that papers on organophosphate toxins had been published in the international scientific press for decades, and so there was no reason to believe that the Allies did not have nerve agents of their own. This belief was reinforced by the fact that all mention of organophosphate toxins had disappeared from the American scientific press at the start of the war. They believed that the disappearance was due to military censorship.

They were right, but the organophosphate toxin that the Americans were trying to de-emphasize was the insecticide DDT, which had been developed in Switzerland just before the war and was strategically important, particularly for military operations in tropical regions. Ironically, the British actually discovered compounds applicable as nerve agents while experimenting with DDT but had failed to clearly appreciate their importance.

British prime minister Winston Churchill made it very clear to Hitler that if Britain were attacked with poison gas, the British would saturate German cities with gas in retaliation. The Allied strategic bombing force was much stronger than Germany's, the Allies were clearly seizing air superiority over Germany, and Hitler had every reason to believe that if he used nerve agents on Britain the Allies would strike back 10 times as hard. Both the Germans and the British believed that they held parity in chemical warfare, and neither Churchill nor Hitler realized that Germany had the upper hand.

Churchill had little reservations about using chemical weapons. To him, they were just another weapon, despite the fact that Britain had signed and ratified the Geneva Protocol. During the desperate days of 1940, when Britain was facing a German invasion, Churchill had energetically built up an arsenal of chemical weapons to greet German troops on England's shores. Even after the threat of invasion faded, the British continued heavy production of chemical weapons.

In the summer of 1944, the Germans began firing at London with their V-1 missiles armed with conventional warheads. The guidance system of the flying bombs was very primitive, and they came down almost anywhere. Most of those killed and injured were civilians who just had the bad luck to be where a flying bomb decided to fall. Churchill was enraged at the indiscriminate attacks and wanted to retaliate by bombarding German cities with chemical weapons from the air.

Churchill's outrage was understandable, given the deaths and injuries of British civilians, but a little hypercritical. The British Royal Air Force's Bomber Command had been pounding German cities for years, and these raids were often all but indiscriminate. The V-1 flying bomb and the V-2 ballistic missile were frightening and destructive, but their effect did not compare to the devastation poured out by Allied 1,000-bomber raids.

While Churchill was very strongly in favor of using chemical weapons, British military planning staffs investigated and recommended against their use. Their objections were not on grounds of humanity but simply because the relatively crude weapons available to the British would have required many more bomber payloads to be as effective as the conventional bombs that were in use.

Churchill reluctantly gave up the idea, which is just as well considering the possible German response. The German had actually done design work on chemical warheads for the V-1, and dozens of flying bombs armed with tabun warheads falling on London every day could have rendered the city a poisoned desert.

As the Allies closed in from west and east, Germany's position became desperate. The pressure on the Germans to use anything that they could to fight back increased tremendously, but even under those conditions they did not use chemical weapons. Allied superiority was great, and the Reich was stretched to the limits. Use of chemical weapons might have gained the Germans a short-term advantage, but the overwhelming retaliation that Hitler had every reason to expect would likely only accelerate defeat.

The United States had never ratified the Geneva Protocol, but President Roosevelt thought that chemical agents were a barbarous weapon. He had no intention of authorizing its use, much to the dismay of the U.S. Chemical Warfare Service (CWS). The American chemical weapons program thrived only because of fear of Japanese chemical warfare capabilities. Newspapers often printed reports of Japanese use of chemical weapons against the Chinese, and Roosevelt issued stiff public warnings that if the Axis used chemical weapons on American troops, they could expect massive retaliation in kind.

Even before the United States formally entered the war, the Americans were discreetly shipping phosgene to the British. Once war was formally declared, the CWS received massive new funding, reaching $1 billion in 1942. Huge new production facilities were built, most notably, the Pine Bluff Arsenal in Arkansas and the Rocky Mountain Arsenal near Denver, Colorado. The CWS also opened a huge test range in Utah, named the Dugway Proving Ground, where there was plenty of space to test biochemical weapons on duplicates of German and Japanese buildings.

Despite the reluctance of the Americans to use chemical weapons, they nonetheless were stockpiling massive amounts of chemical weapons for such an eventuality. With the amount of stockpiling it was only a matter of time before an accident occurred.

On 2 December 1943, the merchant ship SS John Harvey was waiting its turn to be unloaded at the harbor of Bari in southern Italy. The classified cargo of the John Harvey was 2,000 of 45-kilogram (100-pound) bombs full of mustard gas. Only several officers of the merchant ship knew of the cargo.

The Allies believed that they had obtained complete air superiority over southern Italy. They hadn't informed the Luftwaffe of this, and that evening 100 JU-88 bombers swept in and raised hell for 20 minutes. The German raid was a stunning success; it sank 17 ships, badly damaged 8 more, killed 1,000 men, and injured 800. Gas bombs on the John Harvey ruptured, and as the ship sank, a layer of mustard gas and oil spread over the harbor while mustard gas fumes swept ashore in a billowing cloud. Many civilians died during and after the raid.

The officers in charge of the classified shipment on the John Harvey had been killed while they frantically tried to scuttle the vessel, and nobody else knew about the gas bombs. Sailors were taken ashore to a hospital where they were wrapped in blankets and given tea. The next morning 630 of them were blind and developing hideous chemical burns. Within two weeks, 70 of them died.

The crew of a U.S. Navy destroyer, the USS Bistera, picked up survivors during the raid and escaped to sea. During the night almost the entire crew went blind, and many developed burns. The destroyer managed to limp into Taranto harbor with great difficulty.

At first, the Allied high command tried to conceal the disaster, since the evidence that chemical weapons were being shipped into Italy might convince the Germans that the Allies were preparing to use chemical weapons and provoke the Germans into preemptively using chemical weapons themselves. However, there were far too many witnesses to keep the secret, and in February the U.S. Chiefs of Staff issued a statement admitting to the accident and emphasizing that the United States had no intention of using chemical weapons except in retaliation to first use by the Axis powers.

Information on Russian chemical warfare development during World War II and after is sketchy. The Russians presumably manufactured their own substantial stockpiles of chemical weapons, but if so, they kept it a tight secret.

One thing is known. When the Soviets advanced on the Nazi nerve gas plant at Dyenfurth in August 1944, large quantities of liquid nerve agents were poured into the Oder, and the factory was set up for demolition, but the Red Army got there before the charges could be set off. The Dyenfurth plant was dismantled and carted off to Russia to begin production for Stalin instead of Hitler. The Russians now had the secret of tabun, sarin, and a new, even deadlier nerve agent named soman that the Germans had discovered a few months earlier.

The British and Americans also studied captured nerve agent shells and interrogated captured German chemists, most of whom fled west rather than face capture by the Russians. The discovery that the Allies had been completely ignorant of the existence of nerve agents was a shock to Allied intelligence and leadership.

The reluctance to use chemical weapons in World War II remains puzzling. All the major combatants had large stocks of chemical weapons, and some of them available in quantity were vastly superior to those used in World War I. Most believed that chemical weapons would be used, and most had incentives to use them at one time or another.

1945–1970

When the war ended, many of the chemical weapons that were stockpiled were loaded onto old ships, taken out to the deep sea, and scuttled. The disposal of such large quantities of chemical weapons was widely publicized.

The end of the World War II saw the beginning of the Cold War, and research and development into the new nerve agents became a deep secret and high priority on both sides of the Iron Curtain. The Americans, British, and Canadians formed a three-way alliance called the Tripartite Agreement to investigate and develop techniques of chemical warfare with the new "G agents" ("GA" for tabun, "GB" for sarin, and "GD" for soman), as the German nerve agents were known. The Australians joined this alliance in 1965.

The British performed a series of experiments, mostly focusing on GB, through the late 1940s and 1950s. They never went into full production of nerve gases, though they did construct an experimental pilot plant. The British had historical reasons for disliking gas weapons, and besides, the war had exhausted Britain's financial resources.

The Americans had no such obstacles and went into mass production of GB. The CWS, now known as the U.S. Army Chemical Corps, built a plant in Alabama to manufacture the chemical precursors and then finished production at the Rocky Mountain Arsenal. The Dugway Proving Ground, which had been shut down after the war, was reopened in 1950 and expanded for chemical and biological weapon tests.

By the early 1960s, the United States had a huge arsenal of chemical weapons and in fact had begun production of a new chemical agent, designated VX. In 1952, Dr. Ranajit Ghosh of Britain's Imperial Chemical Industries discovered what would become VX while performing research into pesticides. Similar agents were discovered in other countries at roughly the same time.

The older G agents were volatile and tended to evaporate rapidly, while VX, in contrast, had the viscosity of motor oil and, like mustard gas, would puddle up on the ground after an attack and remain there. VX was persistent and much more toxic than GB.

Under the pressure of broad moral scruples and specific economic problems, the British renounced offensive chemical warfare in 1956. However, they passed on the secret of VX to the Americans, who opened a plant in Newport, Indiana, to produce VX in volume. By 1967, the Americans had thousands of tons of VX.

Other work was performed on delivery systems, including artillery shells, the M23 chemical land mine, the M55 unguided chemical rocket, and the MK116 Weteye air-dropped chemical bomb. Defensive systems were not ignored, either, with development of new gas masks, protective clothing, decontamination systems and kits, and primitive detection systems. Nerve agent antidotes, such as atropine, were also developed, and atropine hypodermic autoinjector kits were produced in quantity.

The Americans also investigated chemical agents based on hallucinogens. In 1943, a researcher named Dr. Albert Hoffman at the Sandoz drug firm in Switzerland was investigating drugs derived from ergot, a fungus that infects wheat, when he spontaneously went into wild hallucinations. Dr. Hoffman had accidentally discovered the hallucinogenic drug LSD.

In the postwar period, the Chemical Corps wondered if hallucinogens might make effective "humane" weapons that would not kill enemy soldiers but simply eliminate their will to fight. During the mid-1950s, experiments were conducted on volunteers, as well as unwitting patients in psychiatric institutions, with mind-altering drugs.

The results of these tests were encouraging, but LSD itself was not appropriate for military use. It was much too expensive to synthesize and could not be used effectively as an aerosol. The army finally found a substance named BZ that was cheap, and could be dispersed in clouds over the battlefield. BZ made its victims somewhat ill, causing them to vomit or stagger around. They might suffer memory lapses and hallucinations. Effects could persist for up to two weeks.

BZ was produced in pilot quantities, but then the army had second thoughts. An enemy soldier on hallucinogens was just as likely to do suicidally crazy and dangerous things as become happy and agreeable, and the army didn't want to use such an unpredictable weapon. BZ was discarded.

The U.S. military did use "less lethal" chemical agents in Vietnam, for example, a riot agent named CS, which had been developed by the British during the 1950s as a more potent replacement for traditional tear gas. CS was an aerosol powder and a powerful irritant that attacked the eyes, nose, and throat and burned the skin. In 1965, the Americans began using CS to flush Vietcong (VC) guerrillas out of their hiding holes in the ground and eventually used it in large quantities.

The Americans were accused of conducting chemical warfare with the use of herbicides and CS, and a legalistic argument followed. The critics conceded that the chemicals used were not in the same league as traditional poison gases, much less nerve agents, but pointed out that use of such nonlethal agents was a step that could quickly escalate toward the use of nastier poisons and establish a dangerous precedent. In fact, rumors have persisted that the Americans tested lethal chemical weapons in combat during the Vietnam War, but no substantial evidence has ever been found to back up these rumors.

The controversy over the American use of nonlethal chemical weapons in Vietnam helped keep the fact that the United States had large stockpiles of lethal chemical weapons in the international spotlight. World opinion was solidly against chemical weapons, and there was no way that the Americans could use poison gases, except in retaliation. The U.S. government soon found its stockpiles of chemical weapons an embarrassment. The United States had nuclear deterrence, making the need for lethal chemical weapons arguable.

To further this argument, a rather frightening incident occurred. On 13 March 1968, an F-4 Phantom strike aircraft performed a test mission over the Dugway Proving Ground with chemical dispensers containing VX. One of the dispensers wasn't completely empty. As the F-4 gained altitude after its bombing run, VX trickled out in a trail behind the aircraft, drifting into Skull Valley just north of the proving ground and settling over a huge flock of sheep.

Six thousand sheep were killed, and the incident provoked national attention at a time of high public political unrest and suspicion of the government. In the summer of 1969, a leaky VX munition stored at a U.S. military installation on Okinawa sent 23 servicemen to the hospital. The Japanese government had not even known that chemical weapons were being stockpiled on Japanese soil.

In 1970, President Richard M. Nixon announced a moratorium on the development and production of new chemical weapons, though work on defensive measures continued. The United States finally ratified the 1925 Geneva Protocol in 1975 and the next year began discussions with the USSR on additional measures to limit chemical weapons. However, chemical weapons showed no sign of disappearing.

1970-2000

While the details remain hidden, the Soviet Union engaged in a chemical weapons buildup that almost certainly matched that of the Americans. It seemed that the Soviets had a particular liking for soman/GD and were believed to have developed a nerve agent that could work under extremely cold conditions. Clearly the Red Army possessed a strong chemical warfare component.

The government of Yemen was suspected of using chemical weapons provided by the USSR in the 1960s, and in the mid-1970s reports began to trickle out of Southeast Asia that the Vietnamese, another Soviet ally, were using a new and savagely effective chemical agent in attacks on Hmong tribesmen in Laos, who had been allies of the Americans and stubborn foes of the Communists.

Refugees spoke of aircraft pouring out a "yellow rain" that caused choking, chemical burns, massive bleeding, and rapid death. There were many reports, but the combination of symptoms reported did not match the action of any known chemical agent. U.S. Army scientists suspected that the "yellow rain" was some mix of chemical agents or a new chemical or biological toxin.

The idea that "yellow rain" was some biological toxin was given a little weight in 1981, when a leaf and a few other plant fragments that were covered with a white mold were examined. The mold had a very high concentration of fungal poisons known as mycotoxins. However, the Soviets and Vietnamese denied that they were using chemical or biological warfare in Laos. The evidence was thin at best, and the mycotoxins discovered, while deadly, were nowhere nearly as toxic as any nerve gas and much more expensive to produce. In the absence of any definitive information, "yellow rain" was nothing more than an unsettling rumor.

In the meantime, talks with the Soviets on chemical weapons limitation had bogged down over issues of verification and enforcement. Chemical warfare advocates in the United States, suspicious that the Soviets were using the talks as a mask for improving their chemical warfare capability, challenged Nixon's moratorium on the development and production of new chemical weapons.

The environmental and safety concerns that had, in good part, led to the moratorium were an obstacle to the production of new chemical weapons, but a new concept in chemical weapons developed: binary nerve agents. Back in the 1950s, the U.S. Navy had been concerned about the problem of storing nerve agents on board ships and had investigated a concept where a nerve agent munition would contain two chemical "charges."

The first charge would be stored separately from the munition, which contained the second charge. When the munition was readied for use, the first charge would be plugged in, and the munition fired. A small explosive charge would rupture the containers storing the two charges, causing them to mix and synthesize the desired nerve agent, which would be dispersed when the munition burst.

Research with binary nerve agent weapons in the following decades produced a range of munitions that could deliver GB or VX. The U.S. Defense Department developed a plan for fielding binary nerve agent weapons, but even with suspicion of Soviet intentions and actions, the U.S. Congress showed no inclination to fund the program.

The suspicions continued to grow. The USSR intervened in the civil war in Afghanistan late in 1979, and reports from Afghan rebels indicated that the Soviets were using chemical weapons. Although the rebels spoke of "nerve gas," they described clouds of colored smoke and choking symptoms that sounded more like those caused by asphyxiants. As mentioned earlier, nerve agent are generally odorless and colorless and cause convulsions and suffocation.

The reports were never confirmed. It seems plausible that riot agents were used in Afghanistan, and riot agents can be lethal in high concentrations. The reports from Afghanistan, as well as the "yellow rain" stories from Laos provided little real evidence of any serious Soviet use of chemical weapons.

By that time, however, the Soviets were not the only issue. There was widespread suspicion that lesser states with militant and authoritarian regimes were developing chemical and biological weapons as a military equalizer. That became absolutely clear after the beginning of the Iran–Iraq War in 1980. The Iraqis, badly outnumbered, used mustard gas and possibly nerve agents to spearhead attacks on Iranian forces. Chemical weapons appear to have been a contributing factor to the eventual defeat of Iran in 1988.

After the war with Iran was over, Iraq's Saddam Hussein used his chemical weapons to deal with rebellious Iraqi Kurds who had been assisted by the Iranians. The Iraqis used mustard gases, possibly combined with nerve agents, against a Kurdish town in 1988, killing thousands of people.

During the Gulf War in 1991, there were widespread fears that Saddam Hussein would use his chemical and biological weapons on Coalition forces. He did not, apparently out of fear of retaliation. After the defeat of Iraqi forces, United Nations (UN) inspection teams destroyed many of Iraq's chemical and biological weapons stockpiles, but it proved impossible to determine if all the stockpiles had been found.

The U.S. Army still maintains serious research into biochemical warfare defenses. U.S. military forces are equipped to deal with such attacks and incorporate simulated biochemical weapon attacks into their training. Handheld and vehicle-mounted chemical agent detection instruments are available and used in field operations.

Advanced defensive technologies under development include vaccines to protect soldiers against nerve agents and "hyperspectral imaging" (HSI) sensors to allow the remote detection of chemical agents from small robotic aircraft. HSI sensors have demonstrated that they may be able to give advance warning of chemical weapon attacks, though such sensors have so far not been able to distinguish dangerous biological agents from, say, airborne pollen.

Biochemical warfare remains a potential reality for the U.S. military, and the experience with Iraq did not encourage the idea that the chemical weapons genie could ever be put back in the bottle. However, with the collapse of the Soviet Union, a significant step forward was taken.

The Russian Federation that emerged from the collapse of the USSR had no money to pursue chemical weapons development, and the chemical weapons stockpiles on its territory were a dangerous environmental liability. Under such conditions, the Russians and Americans came to an agreement in 1992 to destroy their chemical weapons stockpiles.

Putting this commitment into action proved difficult for the Americans. The traditional means of disposing of chemical weapons was to put them on old cargo ships, take the ships out to the deep sea, and sink them. This practice was continued into the 1950s, with ships sunk everywhere from the Baltic to the Pacific, but with the rise of environmental consciousness scuttling had become a completely unacceptable measure by the 1960s. In fact, a number of fishermen were injured every year while trawling in waters where chemical weapons had been discarded when they came into contact with crusted clots of mustard agent containers that were stuck in their nets. When the ocean dumping stopped, the number of such incidents declined in the 1970s and faded out.

To compensate for the ban on ocean dumping, the United States built a specialized incinerator on Johnston Atoll in the middle of the Pacific as a pilot plant to demonstrate the safe destruction of chemical munitions. More incinerators were to be built at all of the chemical weapons storage sites in the continental United States for the local incineration of the 33,000 tons of agents stockpiled, since transportation of the agents for destruction elsewhere was ruled out.

The plan, however necessary, proved troublesome. Many of the chemical weapons were becoming leaky and dangerous to store or transport. Opposition from local groups and environmental organizations such as Greenpeace complicated government disposal plans. Initial cost estimates for the disposal of American chemical weapons were in the billions and proceeded to double while schedules slipped well into the next century. A conservative estimate is that disposal will have cost $15 billion in all when it is completed sometime around 2005, and that schedule may be hard to meet.

The Russians, who did not have anywhere near the resources of the Americans, were confronted with an even nastier problem. The Americans have provided funds to help build a chemical weapons incinerator in Russia, which is expected to go on-line in 2003. It will be able to destroy 500 tons of chemical agents a year. As Russian stockpiles are estimated at 40,000 tons, obviously other installations will clearly be required.

In April 1999 it was reported that chemical weapons had been used in the Kosovo crisis. The former federal army of Yugoslavia, JNA, had a rather extensive and highly developed chemical warfare program prior to the breakup of Yugoslavia. The army of the Federal Republic of Yugoslavia (Serbia and Montenegro) has inherited most of the chemical warfare program as well as the stockpiles of chemical agents and equipment.

It has been reported that the Yugoslavian army (VJ) has used the incapacitating agent BZ against opposition forces along the Albanian border. BZ is a incapacitating agent and is intended to produce physiological or mental effects that prevent exposed military personnel from performing their duties for significant periods of time. The VJ Doctrine on the Use of Chemical Weapons advocates the use of this agent against enemy personnel to incapacitate them, then to capture or kill those affected. Current estimates of the amount of this agent in the VJ inventory are in the 300-ton range. In addition, the VJ has produced hand grenades, rifle-propelled grenades, and mortar shells filled with irritants such as CS.

As can be seen, chemical weapons since their inception to this very day are still with us.

CURRENT CHEMICAL WARFARE THREAT

Despite the implementation of the Chemical Weapons Convention (CWC), the number of nations with chemical weapons capabilities has not changed greatly. In addition, those countries with chemical warfare programs are developing new agents and more sophisticated delivery systems. The increase in the research and development of weapons technology, precision navigation technology, and chemical weapons technology of developing nations presents the United States with a complicated national security challenge.

The most effective defense to the developing threat of chemical warfare is intelligence collection and analysis. Keeping current and informed of possible chemical threats allows the United States to develop and update requirements for chemical defense programs.

There are several major regions that currently have the industrial base in which to develop chemical weapons.

Northeast Asia

North Korea's chemical weapons program is believed to be well developed and since 1989 includes the capability to indigenously produce bulk quantities of nerve, blister, choking and blood chemical agents. North Korea is also believed to be in possession of a sizable stockpile of chemical weapons, which could be employed in offensive military operations against South Korea. North Korea also has a well-developed defensive program aimed at protecting its civilian population and military forces from the effects of chemical weapons. Aspects of the defensive program include extensive training in the use of protective masks, suits, detectors, and decontamination systems. Though these measures are focused on a perceived threat, they could also support the offensive use of chemical weapons by North Korea during combat. North Korea has yet to sign the CWC and is not expected to do so in the near term, due to intrusive inspection and verification requirements mandated by the agreement.

China is believed to have an advanced chemical weapons program that includes research and development, production, and weaponization capabilities. It is believed that its current inventory includes a full range of traditional chemical agents. It also has a wide variety of delivery systems, including artillery rockets, aerial bombs, sprayers, and short-range ballistic missiles. Chinese forces, like those of North Korea, have conducted defensive chemical warfare training and are capable of operating in a contaminated environment. As China integrates its defensive chemical warfare training into overall military operations, its doctrine may evolve to reflect the incorporation of more advanced munitions for chemical weapon agent delivery. China has signed and ratified the CWC.

South Asia

India currently has an advanced commercial chemical industry and produces the bulk of its own chemicals for domestic consumption. New Delhi ratified the CWC in 1996. In the required declarations, India has acknowledged that it has a chemical warfare program. New Delhi has pledged that all facilities related to its chemical warfare program would be open for inspection.

Pakistan has a less developed commercial chemical industry than India but is soon expected to have the capability to produce all precursor chemicals needed to develop a chemical weapons program. Like India, Pakistan has numerous munitions systems that could be used to deliver chemical warfare agents, including artillery, aerial bombs, and missiles. Pakistan has ratified the CWC.

The Middle East and North Africa

Iran quickly initiated a chemical weapons program in the early stages of the Iran–Iraq War. The program has received heightened attention since the early 1990s with an expansion in both the chemical production infrastructure as well as its munitions arsenal. Iran currently possesses blister, blood, and choking agents and may have nerve agents as well. It currently has the capability to deliver chemical warfare agents using artillery shells and aerial bombs. Iran has ratified the CWC, declared agents and chemical agent production facilities, and is obligated to open suspected sites to international inspection and eliminate its chemical weapons program.

Iraq had a very well developed chemical weapons program prior to the Gulf War. Its stockpile of chemical agents included a variety of nerve agents, such as tabun (GA), sarin (GB), and GF, as well as the blister agent mustard. From 1985 and continuing uninterrupted until December 1990, Iraq undertook a program to produce the advanced nerve agent VX. Recent United Nations Special Commission (UNSCOM) findings indicate that Iraq has weaponized VX in missile warheads. Although Iraq's chemical warfare program suffered extensive damage during the Gulf War and from UNSCOM activity, Iraq was able to reconstruct key parts of its chemical warfare program. Despite having destroyed over 700 metric tons of agent, UNSCOM is unable to verify Iraqi declarations that it has disposed of chemical precursor, and destroyed all chemical munitions. The nature of Iraq's previous chemical warfare activity and the pattern of denial and deception employed by Iraqi authorities indicate a high-level intent to rebuild Iraq's chemical weapons program.

Syria has a well-developed chemical weapons program, begun in the 1970s, incorporating nerve agents. Future activity will likely focus on chemical weapons development for agent production and storage, as well as possible research and development of advanced nerve agents. Munitions available for chemical warfare agent delivery likely include aerial bombs as well as SCUD missile warheads. Syria has not signed the CWC and is unlikely to do so in the near future.

Libya has had major setbacks to its chemical warfare program, due to intense public scrutiny focusing on its chemical agent production factory at Rabta in the late 1980s and more recently on its Tarhuna underground facility. Regardless, Libya still maintains a small inventory of chemical weapons, as well as a chemical agent production capability. Libya succeeded in producing up to 100 tons of blister and nerve agent at its Rabta plant prior to closing it in 1990. The site was reopened in 1995 as a pharmaceutical plant; however, it is believed that the plant is still capable of producing chemical warfare agents. Libya has not ratified the CWC and is not likely to do so in the near future.

Independent States of the Former Soviet Union

Russia has admitted to having the world's largest stockpile of chemical agents, approximately 40,000 metric tons. This stockpile consists mostly of weaponized agents, including artillery, aerial bombs, rockets, and missile warheads. Agents include a variety of nerve and blister agents. The Russian chemical warfare program is highly developed as judged by the level of sophistication of some its chemical weapons that incorporate agent mixtures and others that have thickeners added in order to increase agent persistence. Russian chemical warfare research has continued, but officials claim that it is for defensive purposes and therefore not within the scope of the CWC. Many of the individual components of the new binary agents developed have legitimate civilian applications and are not incorporated on the CWC's schedule of chemicals.

The threat of proliferation of chemical weapons will certainly increase in the next 10 years. It is expected that countries with existing programs will master the production processes for complete weapons. Countries will become more skilled at incorporating chemical agents into delivery systems and will turn their attention to focusing on battlefield training as well as employment strategy and doctrine. Therefore, the reluctance of some countries to use chemical weapons may be lowered.

A significant increase in the number of government-sponsored offensive chemical warfare programs is not expected. However, the possibility of growing interest in chemical weapons on the part of terrorist organizations should be seriously considered. Simple weaponization of chemical agents does require advanced skills. On the contrary, crude agent dispersal devices could be fabricated by almost any group. Such weapons might be capable of inflicting only limited numbers of casualties; however, they would have significant psychological impact created by fears of chemical agent exposure.

CHEMICAL AGENTS DEFINED

A 1969 report from the United Nations defines chemical warfare agents as "chemical substances, whether gaseous, liquid or solid, which might be employed because of their direct toxic effects on man, animals and plants."[1]

The Chemical Weapons Convention defines chemical weapons as toxic chemicals but also includes ammunition and equipment for their dispersal. A toxic chemical is stated to be "any chemical which, through its chemical effect on living processes, may cause death, temporary loss of performance, or permanent injury to people and animals."[2]

The U.S. Army defines a chemical agent as "substances in either gaseous, liquid, or solid form that is capable of producing incapacitation, injury, or death to exposed personnel."[3]

Biological agents or toxins, poisons produced by microorganisms, are considered chemical warfare agents only if they are used for military purposes. In February 1970 President Nixon announced, "The United States renounces offensive preparations for and the use of toxins as a method of warfare."[4]

The Convention on the Prohibition of the Development, Production and Stockpiling of Bacteriological (Biological) and Toxin Weapons and on Their Destruction of 1972 bans the development, production, and stockpiling of such substances not required for peaceful purposes.

Thousands of chemical substances today are known to be highly poisonous, but only a few are suitable for use as chemical warfare agents. Since first used in 1915, about 70 chemicals have been used as chemical warfare agents. Due to the number of demands that a chemical substance needs to meet in order for it to be considered useful as a chemical agent, only a few exist today.

Some of the criteria that a chemical substance needs to meet include the following but are not restricted to them:

- It must be not only highly toxic but "suitably highly toxic", so that it is not too difficult to handle.

- It must be stable and capable of being stored for long periods without degradation and without corroding the container or packaging material.
- It must be relatively resistant to atmospheric water and oxygen so that it does not lose effectiveness when dispersed.
- It must withstand the heat and pressure that develop when dispersed.
- It must be procurable from raw materials in the quantities required for military use.
- It must be capable of being handled and transported relatively safely.
- It should possess such properties that complete protection from the chemical agent is difficult for the enemy.
- It should minimize the effectiveness of protective equipment.
- The mechanism of action and medical treatment should be known.
- It should also be difficult to detect by normally applied methods prior to onset of physiological and/or psychological effects.

CLASSES OF CHEMICAL AGENTS

Chemical agents can be classified in many different ways. For example, they can be classified by their physical properties (i.e., gas, liquid or solid) or their chemical structure. They also could be classified as to whether they are incapacitating or lethal, or according to their physiological action.

The military, for the most part, have always referred to chemical agents physiological effects on the human body. Over the course of time chemical agents have been classified as one of the following:

- Blister agent
- Blood agent
- Choking agent
- Incapacitating agent
- Nerve agent
- Tear agent
- Vomit agent

Keep in mind that a chemical agent can produce several physiological effects; for examle, a tear agent may also cause an individual to vomit. However, the chemical agent is classified by the effect that it produces in the majority of people.

A brief description of the physiological effects that the different classes of chemical agent have on the human body is listed next. Note that unlike withbiological agents, the onset of medical symptoms is measured in minutes to hours instead of days. In addition, easily observed characteristics such as colored residue, dead foliage, dead insects, and dead animal life are indications that chemical agents have been used.

Blister (Vesicant) Agents—chemical agents that affect the eyes, respiratory tract, and skin, first as a cell irritant and then as a cell poison. Blister agents initially cause irritation of the eyes (and respiratory tract if inhaled), erythema (reddening of the skin), then blistering or ulcerations followed by systemic poisoning. There are three types of blister agents: mustards, arsenicals, and urticiants.

Blood Agents—chemical agents that act upon the intracellular enzyme cytochrome oxidase. Blood agents allow the red blood cells to acquire oxygen but do not allow them to transfer oxygen to other cells. Body tissue decays rapidly due to lack of oxygen and retention of carbon dioxide (first the heart and then the brain are affected).

Choking Agents—chemical agents that irritate the alveoli in the lungs. This irritation causes the alveoli to constantly secrete fluid into the lungs. The lungs slowly fill with this fluid (which is called pulmonary edema), and the victim dies from lack of oxygen (also known as dry land drowning).

Incapacitating Agents—agents that cause physiological or mental effects that lead to temporary disability lasting from hours to days after exposure to the agent has ceased.

Nerve Agents—chemical agents that affect the transmission of nerve impulses by reacting with the enzyme cholinesterase, permitting an accumulation of a stimulator, acetylcholine. Nerve agents affect the voluntary nervous system, parasympathetic nervous system, and the central nervous system. The major effects on the voluntary nervous system are continuous muscle stimulation with uncoordinated contractions, followed by fatigue and paralysis. The effects on the parasympathetic nervous system are pinpointed pupils, bronchial constriction, nausea, vomiting, diarrhea, secretion of the glands of the mouth, nose, bronchi, and gastrointestinal system. The central nervous system is affected with disturbances in thought, convulsions, coma, and lethal depression of the vital centers of the brain.

Nerve agents may be absorbed through the skin, respiratory tract, gastrointestinal tract, and the eyes. However, significant absorption through the skin takes a period of minutes, and prompt medical treatment and decontamination are imperative.

Tear Agents—are compounds that cause a large flow of tears and intense (although temporary) eye pain and irritation of the skin. The effects are immediate but transient.

Vomiting Agents—are compounds that cause irritation of the upper respiratory tract and induce involuntary vomiting. They may also cause coughing, sneezing, pain in the nose and throat, nasal discharge or tears. Headaches often follow.

TYPES OF CHEMICAL AGENTS

Another important factor for a chemical agent is whether it lasts a very short period of time or a lengthy period of time. Depending on the length of time that chemical agents will be a hazard, they are one of the following:

Type A—nonpersistent: an immediate threat that lasts a few minutes and rarely requires decontamination (decon). Type A chemical agents are generally air-contaminating agents and are dispersed as aerosols or vapor clouds with little or no ground contamination.

Type B—persistent: takes a longer time to act and may last for days. In a protected environment, these agents can last for long periods of time. All agents are affected to some extent by the weather. Chemical agents can be decontaminated by the weather. Type B chemical agents are ground contaminating agents and are dispersed in liquid form to contaminate surfaces.

Figure 1.1.
Relative Persistence of Some Chemical Agents

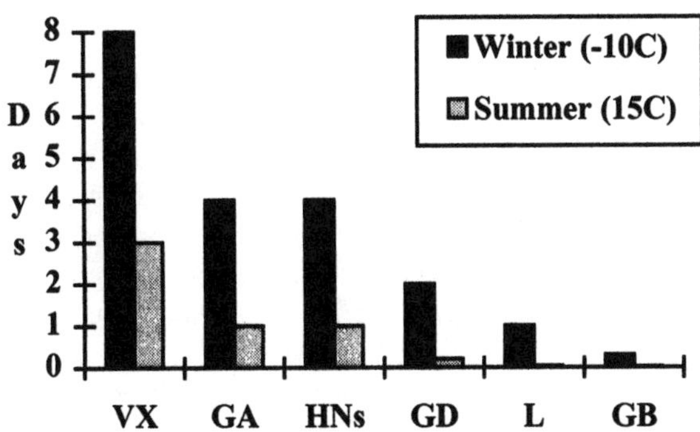

The duration of a hazard is a complex estimation that is based on numerous factors including:

- Type of contamination
- Contamination density and droplet size
- Temperature
- Wind speed
- Sunlight
- Humidity and rain
- Composition of the contaminated surface

- Type of soil and terrain

As can be seen by Figure 1.1, the persistency of several chemical agents can vary greatly depending on several variables, in this instance, the temperature and season. A number of other variables, not solely one variable, must be taken into account when detemining how long a chemical agent is going to persist.

CHEMICAL AGENT CONTAMINATION

Chemical agents can be dispersed by a variety of methods and in a variety of physical forms. The following are the different forms in which chemical agents can be deployed:

- **Solids**—chemical agents that can appear as a fine dust.
- **Liquids**—liquid droplets that fall like rain. Droplets can range from thick and sticky, like syrup, to free flowing, like the consistency of water.
- **Vapors or gases**—created by bursting munitions or generators. These clouds are affected by the weather and can cover large areas.
- **Aerosols**—fine liquids or solid particles suspended in the air. They behave much like vapors and are affected by the weather.

In order to achieve effective ground coverage when a chemical agent is dispersed from a high altitude, the dispersed droplets must be sufficiently large to ensure that they fall within the target area and do not get transported elsewhere by the wind. This can be achieved by the addition of a thickening agent, such as polymers like polystyrene or polyvinylchloride. This results in making them more viscous or thickened. This allows the persistency and adhesive ability to increase, which therefore complicates decontamination.

Although it seems as if chemical agents can be "custom-made" for a specific purpose, this is not the case. A number of variables determine how a chemical agent will act.

The contamination that the deployment of a chemical agent creates can be followed through a series of steps. In brief, once a chemical weapon has detonated, it creates a "primary cloud," which, depending on the chemical agent, can be a solid or liquid aerosol cloud. Factors that affect the hazard from the primary cloud are due to the weather. Factors that decrease the effectiveness of the primary cloud are:

- Variable wind direction, which causes dilution by redirection.
- Wind velocity over 6 meters/sec, which causes dilution by turbulence.
- Unstable air, which causes dilution by turbulence.
- Temperature below 0°C, which causes less evaporation from liquid or solid aerosol particles; aerosol particles settle to the ground more quickly than does agent vapor.

- Precipitation, which washes both aerosol particles and vapors out of the atmosphere.

Factors that increase the effectiveness of the primary cloud tend to be the opposites of those just listed:

- Steady wind direction.
- Wind velocity under 3 meters/sec.
- Stable air (inversion).
- Temperature above 20°C.
- No precipitation.

Once the primary cloud settles, it creates ground contamination. The ground contamination then has a finite lifetime, and a "secondary cloud" of chemical agent can be created by the evaporation of the ground contamination. Eventually the contamination disappears as the chemical agent reacts or is diluted below toxic levels by natural means or decontamination. Factors that will decrease the effectiveness of ground contamination are:

- High ground temperature, which causes decomposition.
- High wind velocity, which causes dilution by turbulence.
- Unstable air, which causes dilution by turbulence.
- Heavy precipitation, which dilutes, hydrolyzes, and washes the contamination into the soil.

Factors that increase the effectiveness of ground contamination are:

- Low wind velocity.
- Stable temperature (inversion).

As noted earlier, the type of chemical agent used helps determine the duration of an area's toxic contamination. Eventually, the contamination disappears as the chemical agent reacts or is diluted below toxic levels. Chemical reactions that affect the persistence of an agent in the environment include:

- Hydrolysis in the environment.
- Photochemical reactions.
- Thermochemical decomposition.
- Reactions with other compounds present in the environment.

Determining the precise lifetime of a chemical agent in the field is very complex. It requires knowing a number of variables for the agent and climate information for the location, including temperature, humidity, rainfall, wind speed, wind direction, and chemical cloud size, among others. Nonetheless, one can assume some average values for temperature, humidity, and rainfall and give approximate lifetimes that indicate the degree of persistence under generalized winter and summer conditions.

TERMINOLOGY

Designation: a two- or three- letter designation used to identify a chemical agent (e.g., GA = tabun) and having nothing to do with the chemical formula or the chemical name of the chemical agent.

Boiling Point: the temperature at which the vapor pressure of a liquid equals the atmospheric pressure. An estimation of the duration of effectiveness (under a given set of conditions) of a chemical agent may be made when its boiling point is known. The vapor pressure and evaporating tendency of chemical agents vary inversely with their boiling points. For example, HD boils at 228°C and evaporates relatively slowly at ordinary temperatures. CG (phosgene)boils at 7.5°C and evaporates rapidly at moderate temperatures.

Flash Point: the temperature at which sufficient vapors of a chemical agent are given off to be combustible when a flame is applied under controlled conditions. The flash point is of interest in the case of chemical agents that have a low enough flash point to cause them to burn when the containing munition bursts.

Liquid and Solid Densities: The density of a liquid chemical agent is the weight in grams of 1 cubic centimeter of the liquid at a specified temperature. The density of a solid chemical agent is the weight of 1 cubic centimeter of the solid at a specified temperature. Liquid or solid density is of interest in computing the chemical efficiency of a munition, since toxicities are always expressed in units of weight. For example, a munition filled with CG, which has a liquid density of about 1.4 g/cm^3 at 20°C, will contain twice as much chemical agent by weight and will have a much higher chemical efficiency than a munition of the same volume filled with hydrogen cyanide (AC), which has a liquid density of about 0.7 g/cm^3 at 10°C. The chemical efficiency of a munition is found by dividing the weight of the filling by the total weight of the filled munition.

Median Lethal Dosage, LD_{50}: The median lethal dosage of a chemical agent employed for inhalation as a vapor or aerosol is generally expressed as the LD_{50}. The LD_{50} of a chemical agent is the dosage (vapor concentration of the agent multiplied by the time of exposure) that is lethal to 50 percent of exposed unprotected personnel at some given breathing rate. It varies with the degree of protection provided by masks and clothing worn by personnel and by the breathing rate. The unit used to express LD_{50} is milligram-minutes per cubic meter (mg-min/m^3). Thus, toxicity tables give for CG an LD_{50} value of 3,200 mg-min/m^3.

Median Incapacitating Dosage, ICt_{50}: The median incapacitating dosage of a chemical agent is generally expressed as the amount of inhaled vapor that is sufficient to disable 50 percent of exposed personnel. For inhalation effect, the median incapacitating dosage is expressed as the ICt_{50}. Incapacitating dosage vary in accordance with the protection provided by masks and clothing worn by personnel and by the breathing rate. The unit used to express ICt_{50} is milligram-minutes per cubic meter (mg-min/m^3).

Melting Point: the temperature at which a solid changes to the liquid state. Because of the low melting point of white phosphorus (WP), a WP-filled munition must be placed on end when stored in temperatures above its melting point so that, on melting, the center of gravity will remain unchanged and thus prevent instability of the munition during flight.

Vapor Density: the ratio of the density of any gas or vapor to the density of air, under the same conditions of temperature and pressure. Vapor density is of some value in providing information as to the probable duration of effectiveness of a chemical agent in valleys and depressions. Diffusion is usually a minor factor in the dissemination of chemical agents, especially after the chemical agent has been diluted by air. Air currents and other influences tend to offset any effects of diffusion or vapor density.

Vapor Pressure: the pressure exerted by a vapor when a state of equilibrium has been reached between the vapor and its liquid or solid state at a given temperature. Vapor pressure is usually expressed in millimeters of mercury (mmHg). It is the pressure that exists in a closed space above the surface of a substance when no other gas, such as air, is present. At any temperature, any substance—liquid or solid—will have some vapor pressure, however small; only when this is appreciable can an ensuing vapor have value as a chemical agent. Vapor pressure is one of the most important properties in considering the tactical usefulness and duration of effectiveness of a chemical agent. However, solid and liquid agents of low vapor pressure may be disseminated effectively as microscopic, airborne (aerosol) particles by mechanical or thermal means.

Volatility: the weight of vapor present in a unit volume of air, under equilibrium conditions, at a specified temperature. The volatility depends on vapor pressure and varies directly with temperature. Volatility is expressed as milligrams of vapor per cubic meter (mg/m^3). Vapor pressure and volatility are related, and vapor pressure is most understandable and useful when it is translated into volatility. Using "T" to express the absolute temperature of the atmosphere, the volatility of a chemical agent may be calculated numerically in milligrams per cubic meter by the following equation derived from the perfect gas law:

$$V = \frac{(mw)(P)(16{,}000)}{T}$$

V = volatility
P = vapor pressure (mmHg at T)
T = temperature (°K)
mw = molecular weight (in grams)

Knowledge of either vapor pressure or volatility is not sufficient to judge the effectiveness of a chemical agent unless the degree of toxicity and physiological action of the chemical agent are also considered. A highly toxic chemical agent of relatively low volatility, such as sarin (GB), may be far more lethal than a less toxic chemical agent of much higher volatility, such as phosgene (CG).

NOTES

1. *Question of Chemical and Bacteriological (Biological) Weapons* (New York: United Nations, 1969).

2. *Convention on the Prohibition of the Development, Production, Stockpiling and Use of Chemical Weapons and on Their Destruction* (New York: United Nations, 1994).

3. *FM 21-41 Soldier's Handbook for Defense against Chemical and Biological Operations and Nuclear Warfare*, (Washington D.C.: Department of the Army, 1967).

4. *FM 3-9 Military Chemistry and Chemical Compounds*, (Washington D.C.: Department of the Army, 1975).

2

Chemical Agents

CHEMICAL AGENT CLASSIFICATION

Table 2.1 references the different types of chemical agents according to the physiological effects that they have on the human body.

The remainder of this chapter lists only the physical and chemical properties of the chemical agents. For a brief list of biological effects, see Chapter 1. For a detailed list of effects, see any standard medical text.

Table 2.1
Chemical Agent Classification

Agent Class	Chemical Agent
Blister Agents	CX, ED, HD, HL, HT, HN1, HN2, HN3, L, MD, PD
Blood Agents	AC, CK, SA
Choking Agents	CG, DP
Incapacitating Agents	BZ
Nerve Agents	GA, GB, GD, GF, VX
Tear Agents	CA, CN, CR, CS, PS
Vomit Agents	DA, DC, DM

BLISTER (VESICANT) AGENTS

Phosgene Oxime—CX

Designation:	CX
Chemical Name:	Dichloroformoxime
Chemical Formula:	$CHCl_2NO$
Molecular Weight:	113.94
CAS Number:	[1794-86-1]
Melting Point:	35–40°C
Boiling Point:	53–54°C
Flash Point:	No data available
Vapor Density:	3.9 (air = 1)
Liquid Density:	No data available
Solid Density:	No data available
Vapor Pressure:	11.2 mmHg @ 25°C (solid) 13 mmHg @ 40°C (liquid)
Volatility:	7.6 x 10^4 mg/m^3 @ 40°C
LCt_{50} (Inhalation):	3,200 mg-min/m^3 (estimated)
ICt_{50}:	No data available
Appearance:	Colorless solid or liquid
Odor:	Sharp; penetrating
Class:	Blister agent
Type:	A—nonpersistent

Structure:

$$Cl_2C{=}NOH$$

Ethyldichloroarsine—ED

Designation:	ED
Chemical Name:	Ethyldichloroarsine
Chemical Formula:	$C_2H_5AsCl_2$
Molecular Weight:	174.88
CAS Number:	[598-14-1]
Melting Point:	-65°C
Boiling Point:	156°C
Flash Point:	No data available
Vapor Density:	6.0 (air = 1)
Liquid Density:	1.66 g/cm^3 @ 20°C
Solid Density:	No data available
Vapor Pressure:	2.09 mmHg @ 20°C
Volatility:	20,000 mg/m^3 @ 20°C
LCt_{50} (Inhalation):	3,000–5,000 mg-min/m^3
ICt_{50} (Inhalation):	5–10 mg-min/m^3
Appearance:	Colorless liquid
Odor:	Fruity but biting; irritating
Class:	Blister agent
Type:	A—nonpersistent

Structure:

$$CH_3CH_2-As\begin{smallmatrix} \diagup Cl \\ \diagdown Cl \end{smallmatrix}$$

Distilled Sulfur Mustard—HD

Designation:	HD
Chemical Name:	Bis(2-chloroethyl) sulfide
Chemical Formula:	$C_4H_8Cl_2S$
Molecular Weight:	159.08
CAS Number:	[505-60-2]
Melting Point:	14.5°C
Boiling Point:	215–217°C
Flash Point:	105°C
Vapor Density:	5.4 (air = 1)
Liquid Density:	1.27 g/cm^3 @ 25°C
Solid Density:	1.338 g/cm^3 @ 13°C
Vapor Pressure:	0.072 mmHg @ 20°C
	0.11 mmHg @ 25°C
Volatility:	75 mg/m^3 @ 0°C (solid)
	610 mg/m^3 @ 20°C (liquid)
	2,860 mg/m^3 @ 40°C (liquid)
LCt_{50} (Inhalation):	1,500 mg-min/m^3
ICt_{50} (Inhalation):	1,500 mg-min/m^3
Appearance:	Yellow to brown oily liquid
Odor:	Mustard vapor is garliclike
Class:	Blister agent
Type:	B—persistent

Structure:

$$Cl—CH_2CH_2—S—CH_2CH_2—Cl$$

HD is H that has been purified by washing and vacuum distillation to reduce sulfur impurities.

H is a mixture of 70% bis(2-chloroethyl)sulfide (HD) and 30% sulfur impurities produced by unstable Levinstein process.

Mustard-Lewisite Mixtue—HL

Designation:	HL
Chemical Name:	Bis(2-chloroethyl) sulfide and chlorovinyldichloroarsine
Chemical Formula:	$C_4H_8Cl_2S$ and $C_2H_2AsCl_3$
Molecular Weight:	186.4, based on the eutectic mixture.
CAS Number:	[505-60-2] and [541-25-3]
Melting Point:	25.4°C -42°C plant purity (calculated)
Boiling Point:	< 190°C decomposes before boiling.
Flash Point:	No data available
Vapor Density:	6.4 (air = 1)
Liquid Density:	1.66 g/cm^3 @ 20°C
Solid Density:	No data available
Vapor Pressure:	0.248 mmHg @ 20°C
Volatility:	240 mg/ m^3 @ -11°C 2,730 mg/ m^3 @ 20°C 10,270 mg/ m^3 @ 40°C
LCt_{50} (Inhalation):	1,500 mg-min/m^3
ICt_{50} (Inhalation):	1,500–2,000 mg-min/m^3
Appearance:	Yellow to brown oily liquid
Odor:	Mustard vapor is garliclike
Class:	Blister agent
Type:	B—persistent

Structure:

$$ClCH_2CH_2{-}S{-}CH_2CH_2Cl$$
$$+$$
$$ClCH{=}CH{-}As{-}Cl_2$$

HL is a mixture of distilled mustard (HD) and lewisite (L) designed to provide a low freezing point for use in cold weather and high altitudes. The eutectic mixture (lowest freezing point) is 63% lewisite and 37% mustard.

Sulfur Mustard—HT

Designation:	HT
Chemical Name:	Bis(2-chloroethyl) sulfide and Bis (2-chloroethylthioethyl) ether
Chemical Formula:	$C_4H_8Cl_2S$ and $C_4H_8Cl_2OS_2$
Molecular Weight:	159.08
CAS Number:	[505-60-2] and [63918-89-8]
Melting Point:	0.0–1.3°C
Boiling Point:	>228°C
Flash Point:	100°C
Vapor Density:	6.92 (air = 1)
Liquid Density:	1.27 g/cm^3 @ 25°C
Solid Density:	No data available
Vapor Pressure:	No data available
Volatility:	831 mg/m^3 @ 25°C
LCt_{50} (Inhalation):	No data available
ICt_{50} (Inhalation):	No data available
Appearance:	Yellow to brown oily liquid
Odor:	Mustard vapor is garliclike
Class:	Blister agent
Type:	B—persistent

Structure:

$$Cl—CH_2CH_2—S—CH_2CH_2—Cl$$

$$+$$

$$ClCH_2CH_2SCH_2CH_2—O—CH_2CH_2SCH_2CH_2Cl$$

HT is a mixture of 60% HD {Bis(2-chloroethyl) sulfide} and 40% T { Bis(2-chloroethylthio)diethyl ether}

Nitrogen Mustard—HN1

Designation:	HN1
Chemical Name:	Bis-(2-chloroethyl)ethylamine
Chemical Formula:	$C_6H_{13}Cl_2N$
Molecular Weight:	170.08
CAS Number:	[538-07-8]
Melting Point:	-34°C
Boiling Point:	194°C (calculated)
Flash Point:	No data available
Vapor Density:	5.9 (air = 1)
Liquid Density:	1.09 g/cm^3 @ 25°C
Solid Density:	No data available
Vapor Pressure:	0.0773 mmHg @ 10°C
	0.25 mmHg @ 25°C
	0.744 mmHg @ 40°C
Volatility:	127 mg/m^3 @ -10°C
	308 mg/m^3 @ 0°C
	1,520 mg/m^3 @ 20°C
	3,100 mg/m^3 @ 30°C
LCt_{50} (Inhalation):	1,500 mg-min/m^3
ICt_{50} (Dermal):	9,000 mg-min/m^3
Appearance:	Colorless to pale yellow, oily liquid
Odor:	Fishy or musty
Class:	Blister agent
Type:	B—persistent

Structure:

$$CH_3CH_2—N(CH_2CH_2Cl)_2$$

CH₂CH₂Cl / CH₃CH₂—N \ CH₂CH₂Cl

Nitrogen Mustard 2—HN2

Designation:	HN2
Chemical Name:	2,2'-Dichloro-N-methyldiethylamine
Chemical Formula:	$C_5H_{11}Cl_2N$
Molecular Weight:	156.07
CAS Number:	[51-75-2]
Melting Point:	-65°C to -60°C
Boiling Point:	75°C @ 15 mmHg
Flash Point:	No data available
Vapor Density:	5.4 (air = 1)
Liquid Density:	1.15 g/cm^3 @ 20°C
Solid Density:	No data available
Vapor Pressure:	0.130 mmHg @ 10°C
	0.290 mmHg @ 20°C
	0.427 mmHg @ 25°C
	1.25 mmHg @ 40°C
Volatility:	1,150 mg/m^3 @ 10°C
	3,580 mg/m^3 @ 25°C
	5,100 mg/m^3 @ 30°C
	10,000 mg/m^3 @ 40°C
LCt_{50} (Inhalation)	3,000 mg-min/m^3
ICt_{50} (Dermal):	6,000–9,500 mg-min/m^3
Appearance:	Pale amber to yellow oily liquid
Odor:	Fruity in high concentrations; soapy-fishy in low concentrations
Class:	Blister agent
Type:	B—persistent

Structure:

```
          CH2CH2Cl
         /
CH3—N
         \
          CH2CH2Cl
```

Nitrogen Mustard 3—HN3

Designation:	HN3
Chemical Name:	Tris(2-chloroethyl)amine hydrochloride
Chemical Formula:	$C_6H_{12}Cl_3N$
Molecular Weight:	204.54
CAS Number:	[555-77-1]
Melting Point:	-3.7°C
Boiling Point:	256°C (calculated)
Flash Point:	No data available
Vapor Density:	7.1 (air = 1)
Liquid Density:	1.24 g/cm^3 @ 25°C
Solid Density:	No data available
Vapor Pressure:	0.0109 mmHg @ 25°C
Volatility:	13 mg/m^3 @ 0°C
	121 mg/m^3 @ 25°C
	180 mg/m^3 @ 30°C
	390 mg/m^3 @ 40°C
LCt_{50} (Inhalation):	1,500 mg-min/m^3
ICt_{50} (Dermal):	2,500 mg-min/m^3
Appearance:	Colorless to pale yellow
Odor:	Butter almond
Class:	Blister agent
Type:	B—persistent

Structure:

$$ClCH_2CH_2—N\begin{matrix} ^{/}CH_2CH_2Cl \\ _{\backslash}CH_2CH_2Cl \end{matrix}$$

Lewisite—L

Designation:	L
Chemical Name:	Chlorovinyldichloroarsine
Chemical Formula:	$C_2H_2AsCl_3$
Molecular Weight:	207.32
CAS Number:	[541-25-3]
Melting Point:	-18°C (mix) 1°C (trans) -45°C (cis)
Boiling Point:	190°C (mix) 197°C (trans) 170°C (cis)
Flash Point:	Does not flash
Vapor Density:	7.1 (air = 1)
Liquid Density:	1.89 g/cm^3 @ 20°C
Solid Density:	No data available
Vapor Pressure:	0.22 mmHg @ 20°C 0.35 mmHg @ 25°C
Volatility:	1,060 mg/m^3 @ 0°C 4,480 mg/m^3 @ 20°C 8,620 mg/m^3 @ 30 °C
LCt_{50} (Inhalation):	1,200–1,500 mg-min/m^3
ICt_{50} (Dermal):	No data available
Appearance:	Colorless oily liquid
Odor:	Geranium
Class:	Blister agent
Type:	B—persistent

Structure:

$$ClCH{=}CH{-}As\begin{matrix}Cl\\ Cl\end{matrix}$$

Methyldichloroarsine—MD

Designation:	MD
Chemical Name:	Methyldichloroarsine
Chemical Formula:	CH_3AsCl_2
Molecular Weight:	160.86
CAS Number:	[593-89-5]
Melting Point:	-55°C
Boiling Point:	133°C
Flash Point:	No data available
Vapor Density:	5.5 (air = 1)
Liquid Density:	1.836 g/cm^3 @ 20°C
Solid Density:	No data available
Vapor Pressure:	7.76 mmHg @ 20°C
Volatility:	74,900 mg-min/m^3 @ 20°C
LCt_{50} (Inhalation):	3,000–5,000 mg-min/m^3
ICt_{50} (Inhalation):	25 mg-min/m^3
Appearance:	Colorless liquid
Odor:	None
Class:	Blister agent
Type:	A—nonpersistent

Structure:

$$CH_3—As\begin{matrix} / Cl \\ \backslash Cl \end{matrix}$$

Phenyldichloroarsine—PD

Designation:	PD
Chemical Name:	Phenyldichloroarsine
Chemical Formula:	$C_6H_5AsCl_2$
Molecular Weight:	222.91
CAS Number:	[696-28-6]
Melting Point:	-20°C
Boiling Point:	252-255°C
Flash Point:	No data available
Vapor Density:	7.7 (air = 1)
Liquid Density:	1.65 g/cm^3 @ 20°C
Solid Density:	No data available
Vapor Pressure:	0.033 mmHg @ 25°C
Volatility:	39 mg/m^3 @ 20°C
LCt_{50} (Inhalation):	2,600 mg-min/m^3
ICt_{50}:	No data available
Appearance:	Colorless liquid
Odor:	None
Class:	Blister agent
Type:	B—persistent

Structure:

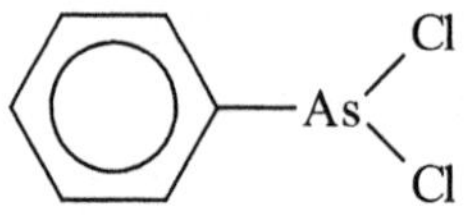

Cl
As
Cl

BLOOD AGENTS

Hydrogen Cyanide—AC

Designation:	AC
Chemical Name:	Hydrocyanic acid
Chemical Formula:	CHN
Molecular Weight:	27.03
CAS Number:	[74-90-8]
Melting Point:	-13.3°C
Boiling Point:	25.7°C
Flash Point:	-18°C
Vapor Density:	0.94 (air = 1)
Liquid Density:	0.687 g/cm^3 @ 10°C
Solid Density:	No data available
Vapor Pressure:	742 mmHg @ 25°C
Volatility:	37,000 mg/m^3 @ -40°C 1,080,000 mg/m^3 @ 25°C
LCt_{50} (Inhalation):	2,000 mg-min/m^3
ICt_{50}:	No data available
Appearance:	Colorless liquid
Odor:	Bitter almonds
Class:	Blood agent
Type:	A—nonpersistent

Structure:

$$N\equiv C-H$$

Cyanogen Chloride—CK

Designation:	CK
Chemical Name:	Cyanogen chloride
Chemical Formula:	CClN
Molecular Weight:	61.48
CAS Number:	[506-77-4]

Melting Point:	-6.9°C
Boiling Point:	12.8°C
Flash Point:	Does not flash
Vapor Density:	2.1 (air = 1)
Liquid Density:	1.18 g/cm^3 @ 20°C
Solid Density:	No data available
Vapor Pressure:	1,000 mmHg @ 25°C
Volatility:	2,600,000 mg/m^3 @ 12.8°C

LCt_{50} (Inhalation):	11,000 mg-min/m^3
ICt_{50} (Inhalation):	7,000 mg-min/m^3

Appearance:	Colorless gas
Odor:	Pepperlike
Class:	Blood agent
Type:	A—nonpersistent

Structure:

N≡C—Cl

Arsine—SA

Designation:	SA
Chemical Name:	Arsine
Chemical Formula:	AsH_3
Molecular Weight:	77.93
CAS Number:	[7784-42-1]
Melting Point:	-116°C
Boiling Point:	-62.5°C
Flash Point:	No data available
Vapor Density:	2.69 (air = 1)
Liquid Density:	1.34 g/cm^3 @ 20°C
Solid Density:	No data available
Vapor Pressure:	11,100 mmHg @ 20°C
Volatility:	30,900,000 mg-min/m^3 @ 20°C
LCt_{50} (Inhalation):	5,000 mg-min/m^3
ICt_{50} (Inhalation):	2,500 mg-min/m^3
Appearance:	Colorless gas
Odor:	Garliclike
Class:	Blood agent
Type:	A—nonpersistent

Structure:

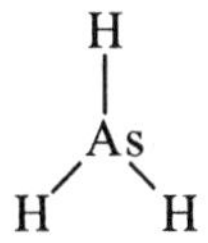

```
    H
    |
    As
   /  \
  H    H
```

CHOKING AGENTS

Phosgene—CG

Designation:	CG
Chemical Name:	Carbonyl chloride
Chemical Formula:	CCl_2O
Molecular Weight:	98.92
CAS Number:	[75-44-5]
Melting Point:	-128°C
Boiling Point:	7.6°C
Flash Point:	Does not flash
Vapor Density:	3.4 (air = 1)
Liquid Density:	1.37 g/cm^3 @ 20°C
Solid Density:	No data available
Vapor Pressure:	1,180 mmHg @ 20°C
Volatility:	528,000 mg/m^3 @ -40°C
	2,200,000 mg/m^3 @ -10°C
	4,300,000 mg/m^3 @ 7.6°C
LCt_{50} (Inhalation):	3,200 mg-min/m^3
ICt_{50} (Inhalation):	1,600 mg-min/m^3
Appearance:	Colorless gas
Odor:	New-mown hay; green corn
Class:	Choking agent
Type:	A—nonpersistent

Structure:

O
Cl—C—Cl

Diphosgene—DP

Designation:	DP
Chemical Name:	Chloroformic acid trichloromethyl ester
Chemical Formula:	$C_2Cl_4O_2$
Molecular Weight:	197.85
CAS Number:	[503-38-8]
Melting Point:	-57°C
Boiling Point:	127 - 128°C
Flash Point:	Does not flash
Vapor Density:	6.8 (air = 1)
Liquid Density:	1.65 g/cm^3 @ 20°C
Solid Density:	No data available
Vapor Pressure:	4.2 mmHg @ 20°C
Volatility:	45,000 mg/m^3 @ 20°C
LCt_{50} (Inhalation):	3,000–3,200 mg-min/m^3
ICt_{50} (Inhalation):	1,600 mg-min/m^3
Appearance:	Colorless liquid
Odor:	New-mown hay; green corn
Class:	Choking agent
Type:	No data available

Structure:

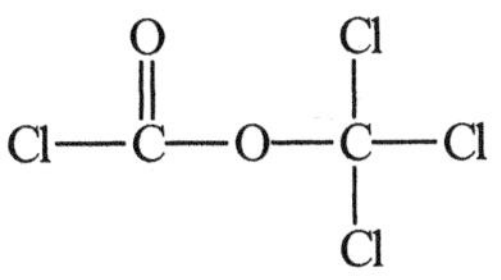

```
        O         Cl
        ||        |
Cl—C—O—C—Cl
                  |
                  Cl
```

INCAPACITATING AGENTS

Agent BZ

Designation:	BZ
Chemical Name:	3-Quinuclidinyl benzilate
Chemical Formula:	$C_{21}H_{23}NO_3$
Molecular Weight:	337.4
CAS Number:	[6581-06-2]
Melting Point:	167.5°C
Boiling Point:	320°C
Flash Point:	246°C
Vapor Density:	11.6 (air = 1)
Liquid Density:	No data available
Solid Density:	1.33 g/cm^3
Vapor Pressure:	0.03 mmHg @ 70°C
Volatility:	0.5 mg/m^3 @ 70°C
LCt_{50} (Inhalation):	200,000 mg-min/m^3 (estimated)
ICt_{50} (Inhalation):	101 mg-min/m^3
Appearance:	White crystalline solid
Odor:	None
Class:	Psychedelic agents
Type:	B—persistent

Structure:

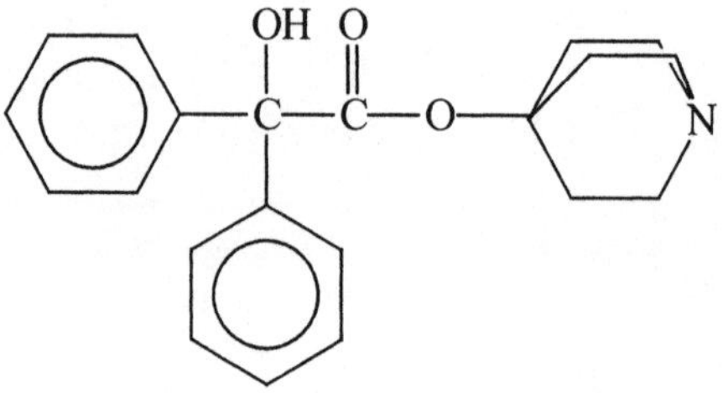

NERVE AGENTS

Tabun—GA

Designation:	GA
Chemical Name:	Dimethylphosphoramidocyanidate
Chemical Formula:	$C_5H_{11}N_2O_2P$
Molecular Weight:	162.12
CAS Number:	[77-81-6]
Melting Point:	-50ºC
Boiling Point:	248ºC
Flash Point:	78ºC
Vapor Density:	5.6 (air = 1)
Liquid Density:	1.07 g/cm^3 @ 25ºC
Solid Density:	No data available
Vapor Pressure:	0.07 mmHg @ 24ºC
Volatility:	90 mg/m^3 @ 0ºC
	610 mg/m^3 @ 25ºC
	858 mg/m^3 @ 30ºC
LCt_{50} (Inhalation):	135–400 mg-min/m^3
ICt_{50} (Inhalation):	300 mg-min/m^3
Appearance:	Clear, colorless liquid
Odor:	Fruity
Class:	Nerve agent
Type:	A—nonpersistent

Structure:

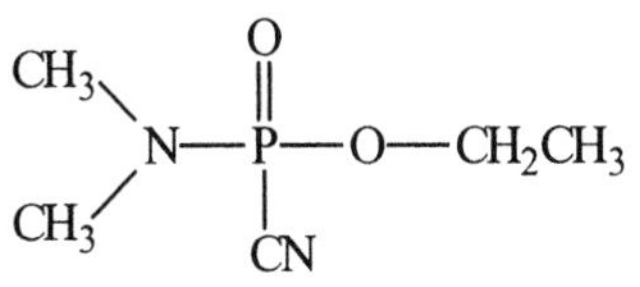

```
                O
CH3\            ||
     N—P—O—CH2CH3
CH3/    |
        CN
```

Sarin—GB

Designation:	GB
Chemical Name:	Isopropyl methylphosphonofluoridate
Chemical Formula:	$C_4H_{10}FO_2P$
Molecular Weight:	140.09
CAS Number:	[107-44-8]
Melting Point:	-57°C
Boiling Point:	147°C
Flash Point:	Does not flash
Vapor Density:	4.86 (air = 1)
Liquid Density:	1.09 g/cm^3 @ 25°C
Solid Density:	No data available
Vapor Pressure:	2.9 mmHg @ 25°C
Volatility:	4,100 mg/m^3 @ 0°C
	22,000 mg/m^3 @ 25°C
	29,800 mg/m^3 @ 30°C
LCt_{50} (Inhalation):	70–100 mg-min/m^3
ICt_{50} (Inhalation):	35–75 mg-min/m^3
Appearance:	Clear, colorless liquid
Odor:	None
Class:	Nerve agent
Type:	A—nonpersistent

Structure:

```
       O
       ||
F—P—O—CH—CH3
       |       |
      CH3    CH3
```

Soman—GD

Designation:	GD
Chemical Name:	Methylphosphonofluoridic acid, 1,2,2-trimethyl propyl ester
Chemical Formula:	$C_7H_{16}FO_2P$
Molecular Weight:	182.19
CAS Number:	[96-64-0]
Melting Point:	-42°C
Boiling Point:	198°C
Flash Point:	121°C
Vapor Density:	5.6 (air = 1)
Liquid Density:	1.02 g/cm^3 @ 25°C
Solid Density:	No data available
Vapor Pressure:	0.40 mmHg @ 25°C
Volatility:	531 mg/m^3 @ 0°C 3,900 mg/m^3 @ 25°C 5,570 mg/m^3 @ 30°C
LCt_{50} (Inhalation):	70–400 mg-min/m^3
ICt_{50} (Inhalation):	35–75 mg-min/m^3
Appearance:	Clear, colorless liquid
Odor:	Camphor
Class:	Nerve agent
Type:	A—nonpersistent

Structure:

```
     O            CH3
     ||            |
F—P—O—CH—C—CH3
     |        |    |
    CH3     CH3 CH3
```

Cyclohexyl sarin—GF

Designation:	GF
Chemical Name:	Methylphosphonofluoridic acid, cyclohexyl ester
Chemical Formula:	$C_7H_{14}FO_2P$
Molecular Weight:	180.2
CAS Number:	[329-99-7]
Melting Point:	-30°C
Boiling Point:	239°C
Flash Point:	94°C
Vapor Density:	6.2 (air = 1)
Liquid Density:	1.13 g/cm^3 @ 20°C
Solid Density:	No data available
Vapor Pressure:	0.044 mmHg @ 20°C
Volatility:	438 mg/m^3 @ 20°C
LCt_{50} (Inhalation):	35 mg-min/m^3
ICt_{50} (Inhalation):	No data available
Appearance:	Clear, colorless liquid
Odor:	Sweet, musty
Class:	Nerve agent
Type:	A—nonpersistent

Structure:

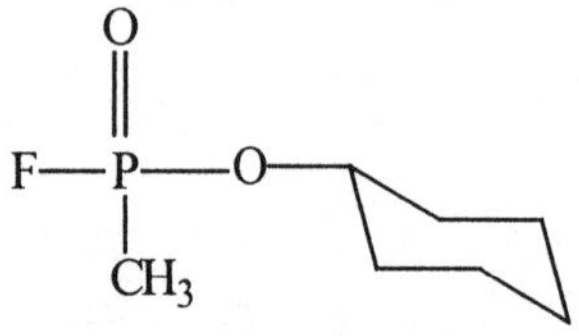

O
‖
F—P—O—(cyclohexyl)
|
CH$_3$

Agent VX

Designation: VX
Chemical Name: Methylphosphonothioic acid, S-[2-[bis(1-methy ethyl)amino]ethyl] O-ethyl ester
Chemical Formula: $C_{11}H_{26}NO_2PS$
Molecular Weight: 267.37
CAS Number: [50782-69-9]

Melting Point: <-51°C (calculated)
Boiling Point: 298°C (calculated)
Flash Point: 159°C
Vapor Density: 9.2 (air = 1)
Liquid Density: 1.0083 g/cm^3 @ 25°C
Solid Density: No data available
Vapor Pressure: 0.0007 mmHg @ 25°C
Volatility: 10.5 mg/m^3 @ 25°C

LCt_{50} (Inhalation): 30–100 mg-min/m^3
ICt_{50} (Inhalation): 25–50 mg-min/m^3

Appearance: Clear, oily liquid
Odor: None
Class: Nerve agent
Type: B—persistent

Structure:

$$[(CH_3)_2CH]_2N-CH_2CH_2-S-P(=O)(CH_3)-O-CH_2-CH_3$$

TEAR AGENTS

Bromobenzylcyanide—CA

Designation: CA
Chemical Name: 4-Bromophenylacetylnitrile
Chemical Formula: C_8H_6BrN
Molecular Weight: 196.0
CAS Number: [5798-79-8]

Melting Point: 25.5°C
Boiling Point: 242°C (decomposes)
Flash Point: Does not flash
Vapor Density: 6.7 (air = 1)
Liquid Density: 1.47 g/cm^3 @ 25°C
Solid Density: 1.52 g/cm^3 @ 20°C
Vapor Pressure: 0.011 mmHg @ 20°C
Volatility: 17 mg/m^3 @ 0°C
115 mg/m^3 @ 20°C
217 mg/m^3 @ 30°C

LCt_{50} (Inhalation): 8,000–11,000 mg-min/m^3(estimated)
ICt_{50} (Inhalation): 30 mg-min/m^3 (approximate)

Appearance: Colorless, crystalline solid
Odor: Soured or rotten fruit
Class: Tear agent
Type: No data available

Structure:

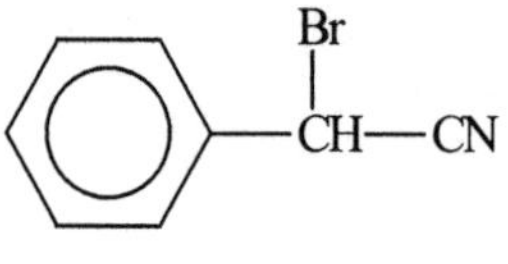

Br
CH—CN

Chloroacetophenone—CN

Designation:	CN
Chemical Name:	Chloroacetophenone
Chemical Formula:	C_8H_7ClO
Molecular Weight:	154.59
CAS Number:	[532-27-4]
Melting Point:	54°C
Boiling Point:	248°C
Flash Point:	118°C
Vapor Density:	5.3 (air = 1)
Liquid Density:	1.187 g/cm^3 @ 58°C
Solid Density:	1.318 g/cm^3 @ 20°C
Vapor Pressure:	0.0026 mmHg @ 0°C
	0.0041 mmHg @ 20°C
	0.152 mmHg @ 51.7°C
Volatility:	2.36 mg/m^3 @ 0°C
	34.3 mg/m^3 @ 20°C
	1060 mg/m^3 @ 51.7°C
LCt_{50} (Inhalation):	11,000–14,000 mg-min/m^3
ICt_{50} (Inhalation):	80 mg-min/m^3
Appearance:	Colorless to gray crystalline solid
Odor:	Floral
Class:	Tear agent
Type:	No data available

Structure:

$$C_6H_5-\overset{\overset{\displaystyle O}{\|}}{C}-CH_2Cl$$

Agent CR

Designation:	CR
Chemical Name:	No data available
Chemical Formula:	$C_{13}H_9NO$
Molecular Weight:	195.25
CAS Number:	No data available
Melting Point:	72°C
Boiling Point:	335°C
Flash Point:	188°C
Vapor Density:	6.7 (air = 1)
Liquid Density:	No data available
Solid Density:	No data available
Vapor Pressure:	0.00059 mmHg @ 20°C
Volatility:	0.63 mg/m^3 @ 25°C
LCt_{50} (Inhalation):	No data available
ICt_{50} (Inhalation):	No data available
Appearance:	Yellow powder
Odor:	Burning sensation
Class:	Tear agent
Type:	No data available

Structure:

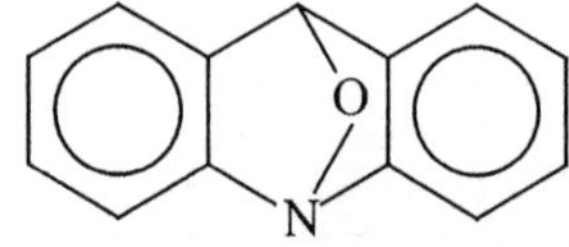

o-Chlorobenzylidenemalononitrile—CS

Designation:	CS
Chemical Name:	*o*-Chlorobenzylidenemalononitrile
Chemical Formula:	$C_{10}H_5ClN_2$
Molecular Weight:	188.61
CAS Number:	[2698-41-1]
Melting Point:	93–95°C
Boiling Point:	310–315°C
Flash Point:	197°C
Vapor Density:	No data available
Liquid Density:	No data available
Solid Density:	1.04 g/cm^3 @ 20°C
Vapor Pressure:	3.4 x 10^{-5} mmHg @ 20°C
Volatility:	0.71 mg/m^3 @ 25°C
LCt_{50} (Inhalation):	61,000 mg-min/m^3
ICt_{50} (Inhalation):	10–20 mg-min/m^3
Appearance:	White, crystalline solid
Odor:	Acrid, pepperlike
Class:	Tear agent
Type:	No data available

Structure:

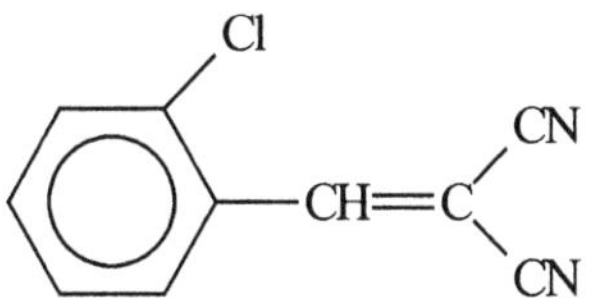

Cl

CH=C(CN)CN

Chloropicrin—PS

Designation:	PS
Chemical Name:	Trichloronitromethane
Chemical Formula:	$CCl_3N_2O_2$
Molecular Weight:	164.3
CAS Number:	[76-06-2]
Melting Point:	-69°C
Boiling Point:	112°C
Flash Point:	Does not flash
Vapor Density:	5.6 (air = 1)
Liquid Density:	1.66 g/cm^3 @ 20°C
Solid Density:	No data available
Vapor Pressure:	20 mmHg @ 20°C
Volatility:	55,700 mg/m^3 @ 0°C
	99,000 mg/m^3 @ 10°C
	164,500 mg/m^3 @ 20°C
	210,700 mg/m^3 @ 25°C
	267,500 mg/m^3 @ 30° C°
LCt_{50} (Inhalation):	2,000 mg-min/m^3
ICt_{50} (Inhalation):	No data available
Appearance:	Colorless, oily liquid
Odor:	Stinging, pungent
Class:	Tear agent
Type:	No data available

Structure:

```
        Cl
        |
  Cl—C—NO2
        |
        Cl
```

VOMIT AGENTS

Diphenylchloroarsine—DA

Designation:	DA
Chemical Name:	Diphenylchloroarsine
Chemical Formula:	$C_{12}H_{10}AsCl$
Molecular Weight:	264.5
CAS Number:	[712-48-1]
Melting Point:	41–44.5°C
Boiling Point:	333°C
Flash Point:	350°C
Vapor Density:	9.15 (air = 1)
Liquid Density:	1.387 g/cm^3 @ 50°C
Solid Density:	1.363 g/cm^3 @ 40°C
Vapor Pressure:	0.00036 mmHg @ 45°C
Volatility:	48 mg/m^3 @ 45°C
LCt_{50} (Inhalation):	15,000 mg-min/m^3
ICt_{50} (Inhalation):	12 mg-min/m^3
Appearance:	White to brown solid
Odor:	None
Class:	Vomiting agent
Type:	A—nonpersistent

Structure:

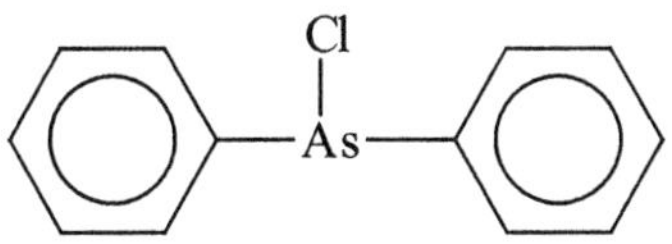

Cl
As

Diphenylcyanoarsine—DC

Designation:	DC
Chemical Name:	Diphenylcyanoarsine
Chemical Formula:	$C_{12}H_{10}AsN$
Molecular Weight:	255.0
CAS Number:	[23525-22-6]
Melting Point:	31.5–35°C
Boiling Point:	350°C
Flash Point:	No data available
Vapor Density:	No data available
Liquid Density:	1.3338 g/cm^3 @ 35°C
Solid Density:	No data available
Vapor Pressure:	0.0002 mmHg @ 20°C
Volatility:	2.8 mg/m^3 @ 20°C
LCt_{50} (Inhalation):	10,000 mg-min/m^3
ICt_{50} (Inhalation):	30 mg-min/m^3
Appearance:	White to pink solid
Odor:	Mix of garlic and bitter almonds
Class:	Vomiting agent
Type:	A—nonpersistent

Structure:

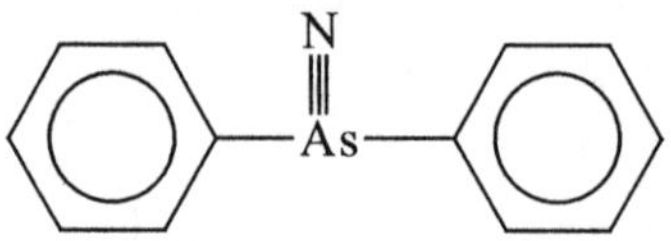

Adamsite—DM

Designation:	DM
Chemical Name:	Diphenylaminochloroarsine
Chemical Formula:	$C_{12}H_9AsClN$
Molecular Weight:	277.57
CAS Number:	[578-94-9]
Melting Point:	195°C
Boiling Point:	410°C
Flash Point:	Does not flash
Vapor Density:	No data available
Liquid Density:	No data available
Solid Density:	1.65 g/cm^3 @ 20°C
Vapor Pressure:	2 x 10^{-13} mmHg @ 20°C
Volatility:	19,300 mg/m^3 @ 0°C
	26,000 to 120,000 mg/m^3 @ 20°C
	72,500 to 143,000 mg/m^3 @ 25°C
LCt_{50} (Inhalation):	11,000 mg-min/m^3
ICt_{50} (Inhalation):	22–150 mg-min/m^3
Appearance:	Yellow to green crystals
Odor:	None
Class:	Vomiting agent
Type:	A—nonpersistent

Structure:

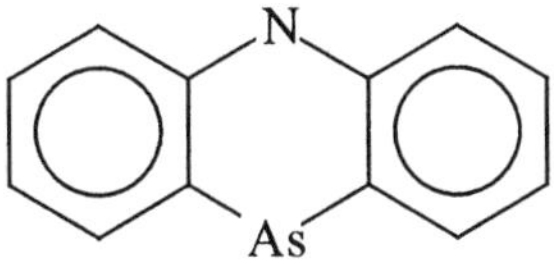

N

As

3

Delivery Systems

CHEMICAL MUNITIONS

The current U.S. chemical weapons stockpiles are located on army bases at eight continental U.S. sites. The locations (see Figure 3.1) and distribution of chemical agents (percentage is by weight of agent) are listed in Table 3.1.

Table 3.1
Percentage of Chemical Agents by Location

Site	Location	Agent	Percentage
1	Aberdeen Proving Ground, MD	HD	5.5
2	Anniston Army Depot, AL	HD, HT, GB, VX	7.6
3	Lexington Army Depot, KY	H, GB, VX	1.8
4	Newport Army Ammunition Plant, IN	VX	4.3
5	Pine Bluff Arsenal, AR	HD, HT, GB, VX	13.0
6	Pueblo Depot, CO	HD	8.9
7	Tooele Army Depot, UT	H, HD, HT, L, GB, VX	46.2
8	Umatilla Depot, OR	HD, GB, VX	12.6
			100.0

Figure 3.1
Locations of Continental Chemical Stockpiles

Note: Numbers refer to site locations in Table 3.1.

The chemical weapon stockpiles include chemical agents stored in bulk containers without explosives and propellants, as well as rockets, land mines, mortars, and artillery projectiles composed of both chemical agents and various explosive propellant components. The total amount of chemical agents contained in the stockpiles has been estimated to be 30,000 tons, although the exact amount is classified. The chemical weapons contain either nerve agents (GB and VX) or blister (vesicant) agents (H, HT, HD, and L); see Chapter 2 for more information.

Most of the stockpile chemical agents are contained in "unitary" or single compound munitions; that is, the munition is filled with a completed chemical agent that is directly toxic to humans, as opposed to "binary" agents that consists of two, relatively nontoxic compounds until the munition is deployed, at which time the two compounds mix and form a chemical agent. The only binary munition manufactured in quantities beyond research and development levels was the 155mm M687 projectile, which formed the GB nerve agent. See later in chapter for more details.

Although the exact number of binary weapons in the U.S. stockpiles is classified, it has been described by the House Committee on Appropriations as "negligible." Most (64.5%) of chemical agents are not contained in munitions but stored in steel,one-ton bulk containers. However, most of the individual chemical weapons in the stockpile are contained in the various munitions as described in Table 3.2.

Table 3.2
Specifications of Chemical Munitions

Munition	Diameter	Length (inches)	Total Weight (lbs)	Chemical Agent	Agent Weight (lbs)
105mm Projectile					
M60	105mm	21.0	32	HD	3.0
M360	105mm	16.0	32	GB	1.6
155mm Projectile					
M104	155mm	26.8	95	H/HD	11.7
M110	155mm	26.8	99	H/HD	11.7
M121	155mm	26.7	100	GB	6.5
M121A1	155mm	27	100	GB/VX	6.5/6.0
M122	155mm	26.7	100	GB	6.5
M687	155mm	---	---	GB	---
8-inch Projectile					
M426	8 in.	35.1	199	GB/VX	14.5
Rocket					
M55	115mm	78.0	56/57	VX/GB	10.0/10.7
Mortar					
M2	4.2 in.	21	25	HD/HT	6.0/5.8
M2A1	4.2 in.	21	25	HD/HT	6.0/5.8
Land Mine					
M23	13.5 in.	5.0	22.75	VX	10.5
Aerial Bomb					
BLU-80 (Bigeye)	13.25 in.	90	595	VX	180
MC-1	16 in.	50	725	GB	220
MK-94	11 in.	60	441	GB	108
MK-116 (Weteye)	14 in.	86	525	GB	347
Spray Tank					
TMU-28/B	22.5 in.	185	1,935	VX	1,356
Ton Container	30.1 in.	81.5 in.	3,100	HD/HT/L	1,700
	30.1 in.	81.5 in.	2,900	GB	1,500
	30.1 in.	81.5 in.	3,000	VX	1,600

Table 3.3
Distribution of Chemical Weapons by Quantity

Chemical Munition	Aberdeen	Anniston	Lexington	Newport	Pine Bluff	Pueblo	Tooele	Umatille	Total
Mustard Agent									
105mm projectile (HD)		23,064				383,418			406,482
155mm projectile (HD)		17,643	15,492			299,554	54,663		387,352
4.2 in projectile (HD)		75,360				97,106	976		173,442
Ton container (HD)	1911*	108			107		6,398	2,635	11,159
4.2 in projectile (HT)		183,552					62,590		246,142
Ton container (HT)					3,591				3,591
Ton container (L)							10		10
	*estimate								
GB Agent									
105mm projectile		74,040					798,703		872,743
155mm projectile		9,600					89,141	47,406	146,147
8 in projectile		16,026	3,977					14,246	34,249
M55 rocket		42,762	51,740		90,409		30,001	91,442	306,354
MK94 (500 lb bomb)								27	27
MC1 (750 lb bomb)							4,463	2,418	6,881
MK116 (Weteye bomb)							888		888
Ton container							5,709		5,709
VX Agent									
155mm projectile		139,581	12,816				53,216	32,313	237,926
8 in projectile							1	3,752	3,753
M55 rocket		35,662	17,733		19,608		3,966	14,519	91,488
M23 landmine		44,131			9,378		22,690	11,685	67,463
Spray tank							862	156	1,018
Ton container				1,690			640		2,330

Table 3.4
Distribution of Chemical Weapons by Weight (in pounds)

Chemical Munition	Aberdeen	Anniston	Lexington	Newport	Pine Bluff	Pueblo	Tooele	Umatilla	Totals
Mustard Agent									
105mm projectile (HD)		68,500				1,150,254	699,540		1,918,294
155mm projectile (HD)		206,420	181,260			3,504,782			3,892,462
4.2 in projectile (HD)		452,160				582,636	5,860		1,040,656
Ton container (HD)	3,250,000	185,080			188,400		11,383,420	4,679,040	19,685,940
4.2 in projectile (HT)		1,064,600					363,020		1,427,620
Ton container (HT)					6,249,100				6,249,100
Ton container (L)							25,920		25,920
GB Agent									
105mm projectile		120,680					1,301,880		1,422,560
155mm projectile		62,400					579,420	308,140	949,960
8 in projectile		232,380	57,660					206,560	496,600
M55 rocket		457,560	553,620		967,380		321,020	978,440	3,278,020
MK94 (500 lb bomb)								2,920	2,920
MC1 (750 lb bomb)							981,860	531,960	1,513,820
MK116 (Weteye bomb)							308,140		308,140
Ton container							8,598,200		8,598,200
VX Agent									
155mm projectile		837,480	76,900				319,300	193,880	1,427,560
8 in projectile							20	54,400	54,420
M55 rocket		356,620	177,340		1956080		39,660	145,200	914,900
M23 landmine		463,380			98,460		238,240	122,700	922,780
Spray tank							1,168,880	211,540	1,380,420
Ton container				2,538,660			910,960		3,449,620
Totals	3,250,000	4,507,260	1,046,780	2,538,660	7,699,420	5,237,672	27,245,340	7,434,780	58,959,912

Table 3.3 shows the breakdown for each stockpile location of the quantity of each type of chemical munition. Table 3.4 shows the breakdown for each stockpile location of the weight of the chemical agent for each type of munition and the total weight of the chemical agents in each location.

ARTILLERY PROJECTILES

105mm—M60 Projectile

The body of this 105mm projectile consists of a hollow one-piece steel forging. A fuse adapter is screwed into the body and brazed in place. The HD mustard blister agent is added and the burster well is then press-fitted into the fuse adapter followed by the M5 tetrytol burster's being installed into the burster well. A fuse well cap, made of either aluminum or Bakelite, is installed by first coating the lower interior threads of the fuse adapter with sealing compound or cement and then screwing the cap down into the fuse adapter. The M60 is then closed by screwing on an M57 or M51A5 point detonating fuse and staking it in place. Staking is an operation in which a punch is used to deform the metal of the fuse so that the metal is pushed into a notch in the projectile body, thereby locking the threaded joint. See Figure 3.2.

Figure 3.2
Cutaway View of 105mm M60 Projectile

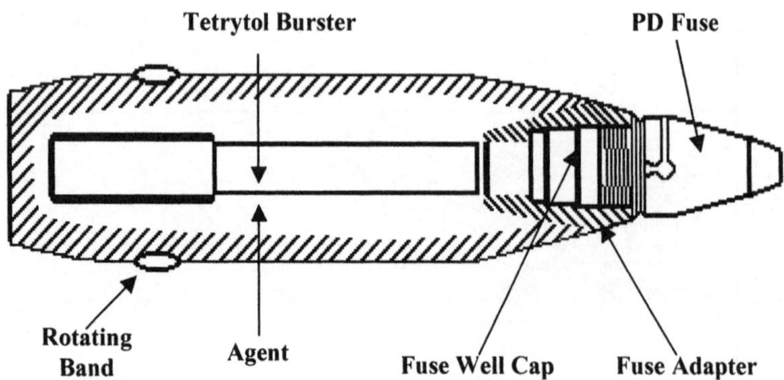

105mm—M84 Leaflet Projectile/M84A1 HC Smoke Projectile

The body of this 105mm projectile consists of a hollow, one-piece steel forging. A fuse adapter is screwed into the body and brazed in place. The

105mm M84 Leaflet Cartridge is currently considered surplus, while the derivative 105mm M84A1 HC Smoke Cartridge remains in active service.

105mm—M360 Projectile

The body of the projectile is cast and finished from low-carbon steel. GB nerve gas agent is added to the interior of the body and sealed inside by press-fitting a steel burster well into the body. The M16 burster casing, containing an M40 tetrytol charge or an M40A1 composition B4 charge, is installed in the burster well. The assembly is completed by screwing an M508 or M557 point detonating fuse into the nose of the projectile and staking it in one or more locations. See Figure 3.3.

Figure 3.3
Cutaway View of 105mm M360 Projectile

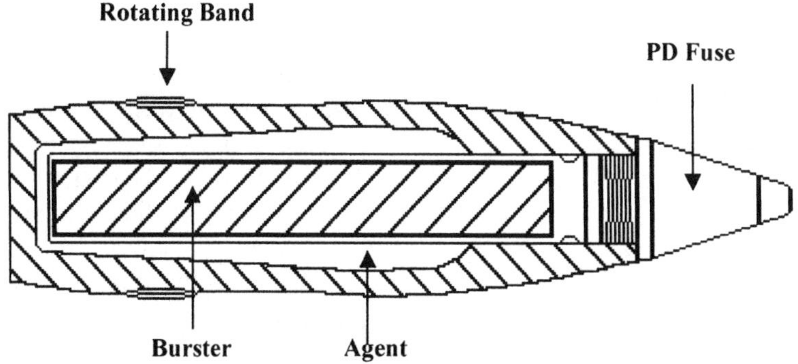

155mm—M104 Projectile

The body of the 155mm M104 projectile consists of a hollow steel shell containing either H or HD blister agent. A fuse adapter is screwed into the body and brazed in place. The agent is added and the burster well is then press-fitted into the fuse adapter followed by the M6 tetrytol burster's being installed into the burster well. A fuse well cap made of either aluminum or Bakelite is installed by first coating the lower interior threads of the fuse adapter with sealing compound or cement and the screwing the cap down into the fuse adapter. The 155mm M104 projectile is then closed by screwing on a lifting plug. See Figure 3.4.

Figure 3.4
Cutaway View of 155mm M104 Projectile

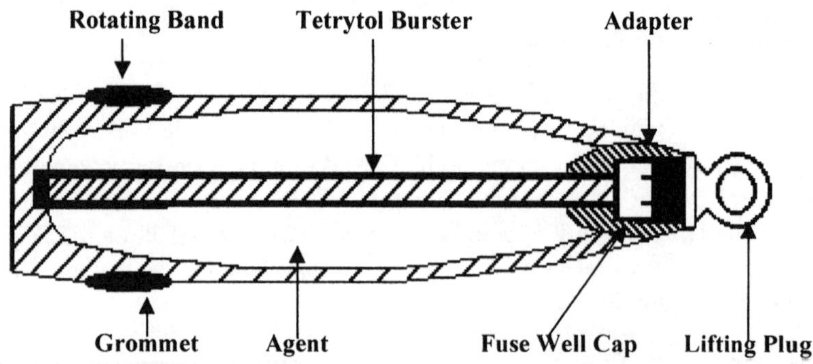

155mm—M110 Projectile

The body of this 155mm projectile consists of a hollow steel shell containing H or HD blister agent. A fuse adapter is screwed into the body and brazed in place. The agent is added, and the burster well is then press-fitted into the fuse adapter followed by the M6 tetrytol burster's being installed into the burster well. A fuse well cap made of either aluminum or Bakelite is installed by first coating the lower interior threads of the fuse adapter with sealing compound or cement and screwing the cap down into the fuse adapter. The M110 is then closed by screwing on a lifting plug. See Figure 3.5.

Figure 3.5
Cutaway View of 155mm M110 Projectile

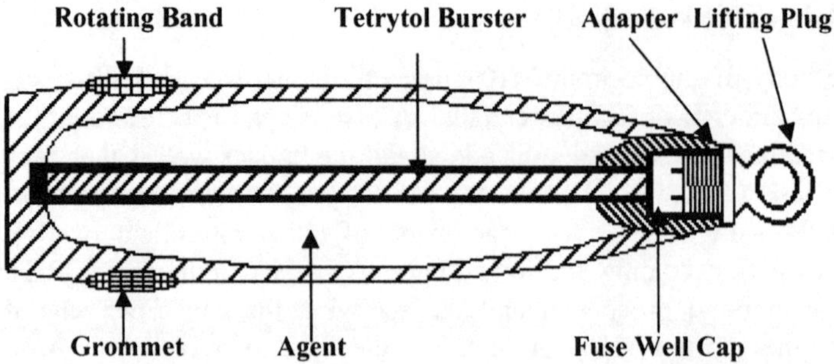

155mm—M121 Projectile

The M121 155mm projectile starts as a hollow steel shell. GB nerve gas agent is added and sealed inside by pressing the burster well into the body. The M37 tetrytol burster is then installed into the burster well. The fuse adapter is screwed in and staked to the body. Next, the lower interior threads of the fuse adapter are coated with sealing compound or cement, and the fuze well cap is screwed down into the fuze adapter. The lifting plug is then screwed into the fuze adapter. The M121A1 can be filled with either GB or VX nerve gas. See Figures 3.6 and 3.7.

Figure 3.6
Cutaway View of 155mm M121 Projectile

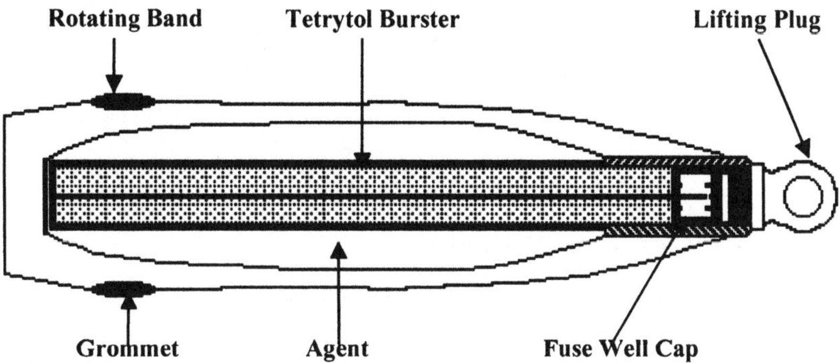

Figure 3.7
Cutaway View of 155mm M121A Projectile

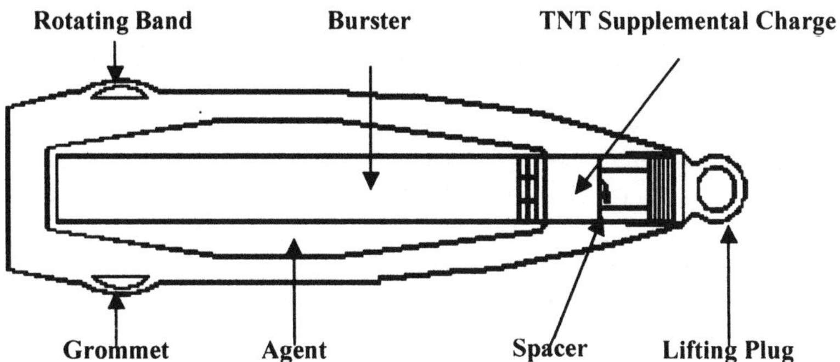

155mm—M122 Projectile

See Figure 3.8.

Figure 3.8
Cutaway View of 155mm M122 Projectile

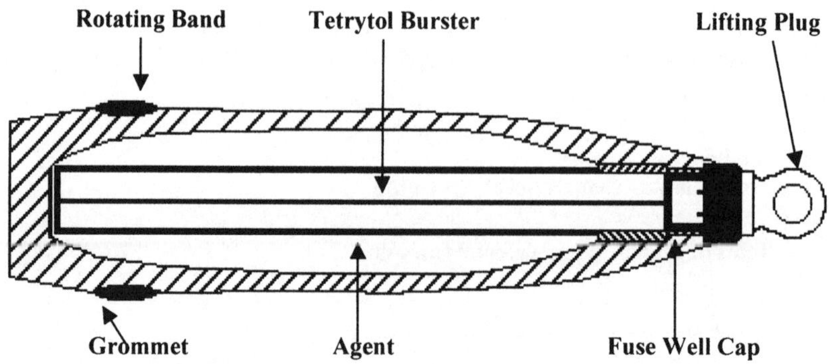

155mm—M687 Binary Projectile

In the 1980s, the army developed binary chemical munitions to replace its aging chemical weapons stockpile. The binary munitions, when fully loaded under battle conditions, consisted of a projectile body and two separate canisters of nonlethal liquid compounds. The two nonlethal liquid compounds, when loaded in the projectile body and fired, would mix, forming a chemical agent enroute to a designated target. The only binary munition manufactured in quantities beyond research and development levels was the 155mm M687 projectile, which formed the GB nerve agent. For national security and safety reasons, the army has always stored the two nonlethal liquid compound canisters in separate locations. Therefore, none of the stored projectiles or canisters contain lethal chemical agents.

The U.S. Army plans to recover and recycle the projectile body and one of the nonlethal compound canisters (designated as the M21 OPA canister). The 155mm M687 projectile and the M21 OPA canister are stored at the Tooele Chemical Depot, Utah, and the Umatilla Chemical Depot, Oregon.

The projectile comprises of a metal body, aluminum explosive casing, and a loaded M21 OPA-filled canister. The M21 OPA-filled canister contains one of the nonlethal liquid compounds of isopropyl alcohol and isopropylamine (the mixture is designated by the acronym OPA).

The Chemical Weapons Convention and its supporting agreements specifically require the disassembly of the 155mm M687 projectile and the M21 OPA-filled canister. The safe recovery and recycling of the 155mm M687 projectile and the M21 OPA canister are the responsibility of the project manager for non-stockpile chemical materiel (PM NSCM). The PM NSCM began the disassembly process in November 1997.

The PM NSCM provides for shipment of the 155mm M687 projectiles and the M21 OPA-filled canisters via a tractor trailer to Hawthorne Army Depot, Nevada. Hawthorne Army Depot, located approximately 140 miles southeast of Carson City, was selected because of its unique capabilities to recover and recycle these various components safely.

The Hawthorne Army Depot recycling and recovery effort consists of three primary steps. First, the M21-OPA filled canister is removed from the projectile, punctured, and drained. The drained OPA liquid is collected in a 55-gallon drum and shipped offsite to an approved treatment, storage, and disposal facility for ultimate disposal. The empty canister is shredded and disposed of in a regulated, solid waste landfill. Next, an abrasive water jet cuts the metal projectile body in two places to enable removal of the aluminum explosive casing. Once the aluminum explosive casing has been separated, all military markings will be removed to allow for sale of the munition body as scrap metal. Finally, a melt-out process removes the explosive from its aluminum explosive casing. Once melted, the explosive is recovered by drying and packaging it for resale and reuse. The empty aluminum casing is smelted into bars and sold for commercial use. See Figure 3.9.

Figure 3.9
Cutaway View of a Binary Projectile

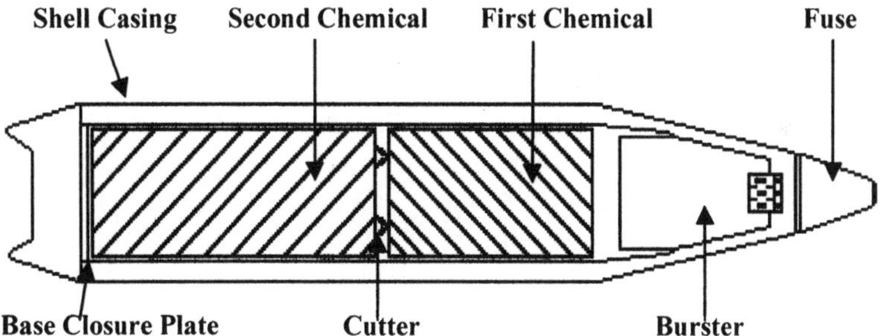

Eight-Inch—M426 Projectile

The M426 eight-inch projectile starts as a hollow steel shell. GB or VX nerve agent is added and sealed inside by pressing the burster well into the body. The M83 burster is then installed into the burster well. The charge support, the TNT supplementary charge, and the spacer are installed, and the fuse adapter/lifting plug is screwed into the body. The adapter is then staked in one or more places. See Figure 3.10.

Figure 3.10
Cutaway View of 203mm M426 Projectile

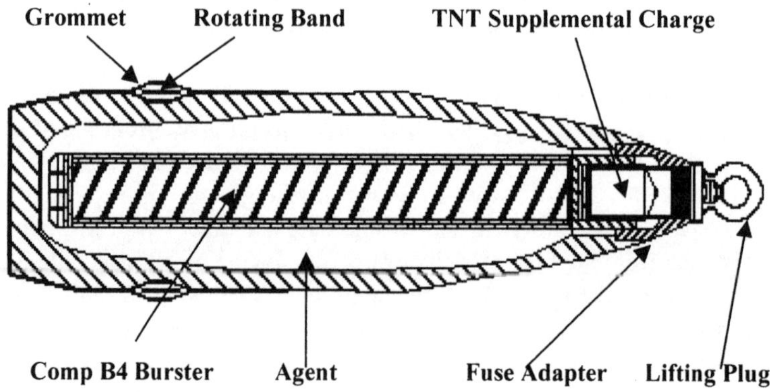

M55 ROCKET

The M55 rocket was produced in the late 1950s to provide toxic chemical offensive capability for large target areas at long range. The rocket was designed for battlefield use and consisted of an aluminum nozzle assembly with spring-loaded fins, a rocket motor, and a fused warhead containing a chemical agent. The M55 rockets can be recognized by three green bands around its body.

The M55 rocket consists of a chemical agent-filled warhead attached to a rocket motor. It has a diameter of 115 millimeters (4.44 inches), is 78 inches long, and weighs 57 pounds. The warhead is filled with either 10.7 pounds of GB or 10.0 pounds of VX. The rocket is stored in a shipping and firing tube. The tube is made of fiberglass-reinforced resin, either epoxy or polyester. The warhead consists of a body, a burster well containing two bursters in series, a fuse adapter, and a point detonating fuse. The rocket motor consists of a body, nozzle-fin assembly, propellant, igniter assembly, and end cap. The propellant is an M28 double base (nitroglycerine and nitrocellulose) cast grain weighing 19.3 pounds.

During the early 1960s, the U.S. Army stored M55 rockets at Black Hills Army Depot, South Dakota. Simulant rockets containing water or ethyl glycol instead of chemical agent were used to train soldiers on the proper handling and firing of the M55. Some of the explosive simulant rockets were used in storage igloo explosion tests, and the remains of some of those rockets were not recovered.

Other sites where the M55 rockets were formerly stored are Rocky Mountain Arsenal, Colorado, and Okinawa, Japan. From Japan, they were later moved to Johnston Atoll in the Pacific. The rockets were originally produced at Newport Army Ammunition Plant, Indiana and were briefly tested at Aberdeen Proving Grounds. However, neither of these locations stored them for extended periods of time.

Congress has mandated a deadline of 31 December 2004, for disposal of the U.S. chemical weapons stockpile. On 23 January 1995, the army released a report to the public on the remaining storage life of the M55 rockets in the U.S. chemical weapons stockpile. As part of the Chemical Stockpile Disposal Program, the army has performed several hazard analyses and risk assessments of continued storage of chemical munitions, including this recent study on M55 rocket propellant stability. These studies were conducted to determine if degradation of munitions and their contents could contribute to an increased risk to the public. The results indicate that the rockets can be safely stored until they are disposed of by the congressionally mandated deadline.

The M55 Rocket Storage Life Evaluation report focused on the rate of deterioration of the propellant found in the approximately 478,000 M55 rockets in the U.S. stockpile. These rockets, containing chemical agent fill, explosives, and propellant, are stored in five locations throughout the United States and at Johnston Island in the Pacific. Those five other locations are Tooele, Utah; Anniston, Alabama; Umatilla, Oregon; Pine Bluff, Arkansas; and Blue Grass, Kentucky. As of March 1997, all rockets at Johnston Island were safely destroyed.

Previous reports predicted the possibility of autoignition, caused by the natural depletion of the propellant stabilizer ranging from 27 to 100 years from the date of manufacture. The stabilizer is a substance that was added to the propellant to slow its degradation. Technical experts, including the propellant manufacturer, used two different methods to estimate the storage life of nonleaking M55 rockets. The most conservative model estimated that there is less than a one-in-a-million chance that a rocket will ignite by itself before the year 2013.

The report cautioned that its conclusions are limited only to nonleaking rockets. There is some evidence that leaking rockets in which the propellant came in direct contact with a chemical agent could have shorter storage lives. The report noted that additional data should be obtained to gain more confidence in the estimate because the samples that were studied may not represent the condition of rockets at all storage locations. An investigation is under way to find out whether propellant exposure to a chemical agent increases the rate of deterioration of the stabilizer itself. The army is currently addressing these issues as part of its Enhanced Stockpile Surveillance Program. See Figure 3.11.

Figure 3.11
Cutaway View of the 115mm M55 Rocket Warhead

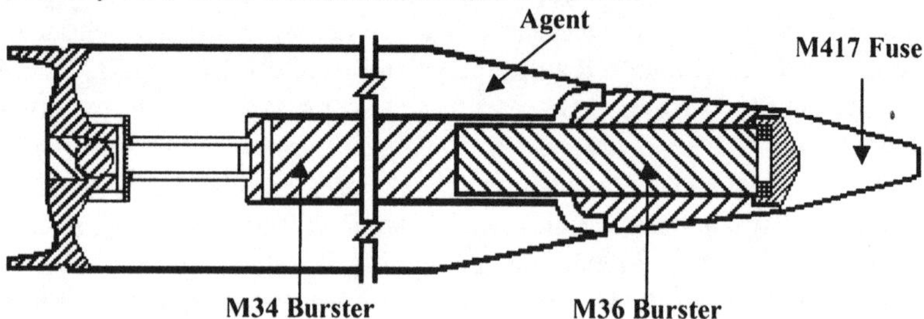

M2 MORTAR PROJECTILE

The 107mm or 4.2-inch M2 mortar projectile contains either HD or HT blister agent. It consists of a one-piece, forged steel case projectile body with fuse, burster, and tail assembly. It has a perforated vane assembly welded to the inside of the body, which is designed to accommodate the burster tube that extends from the fuse. The tail assembly consists of a pressure plate and rotating disk, propelling charge, cartridge container, ignition cartridge, and striker nut assembly. The M2A1 has an aluminum pressure plate, and the M2 has a steel plate. The M8 integral fuse includes the 14.0-inch M14 burster. See Figure 3.12.

Figure 3.12
Cutaway View of 107mm 4.2-inch M2 Mortar Projectile

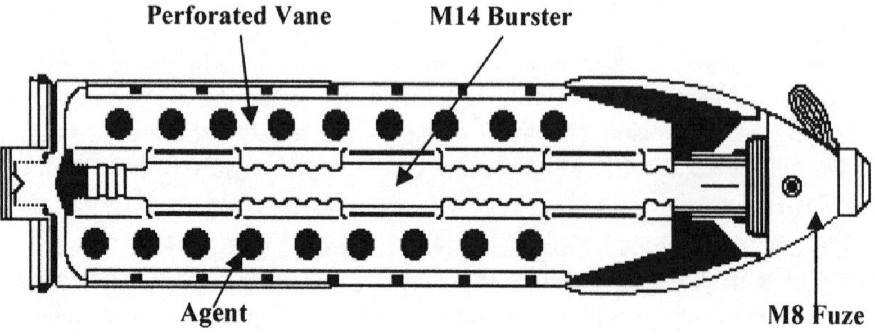

M23 VX LAND MINE

Manufactured after World War II, the M23 chemical land mine was designed to disperse a nerve agent upon explosion. It was designed to be used as an antitank or antipersonnel mine. The M23 land mine is a 13-inch-diameter and 5-inch-high munition filled with 10.5 pounds of VX nerve gas. The mine weighs 22.75 pound unfused. The center of the mine has a three-quarter-pound explosive charge and an activating system designed to rupture the mine and spread its contents. As assembled, the M23 land mines are filled with VX nerve agent and have burster charges in the main fuse well and activator well. See Figure 3.13.

Figure 3.13
Cutaway View of M23 Land Mine

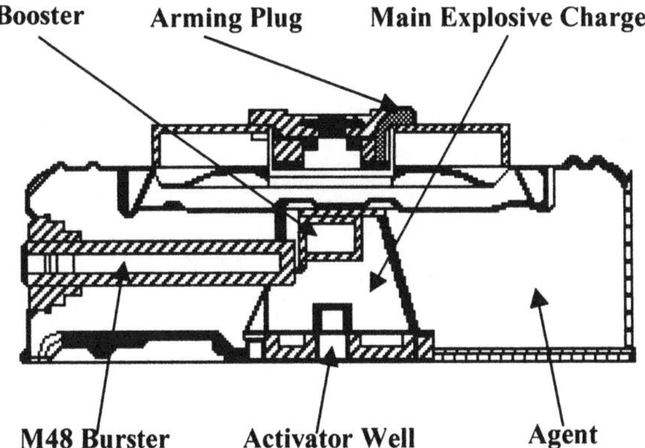

AERIAL BOMBS

BLU-80/B—Bigeye Chemical Weapon

Bigeye is a triservice, safe-to-handle binary chemical air-to-ground weapon. When employed, Bigeye is designed to delay and disrupt airfields, troops, and logistical lifelines by forcing an enemy into a chemical protective posture and to deter adversaries from using their chemical weapons. The Bigeye metal parts contract was awarded in June 1988 for the procurement of production-representative operational test units, trainers, and Safe Separation Test Vehicles. See Figure 3.14.

CHARACTERISTICS

Length:	90 inches
Diameter:	13.25 inches
Wing Span:	17.25 inches
Agent:	VX
Agent Weight:	180 pounds
Total Weight:	595 pounds

Figure 3.14
Cutaway View of an Aerial Bomb

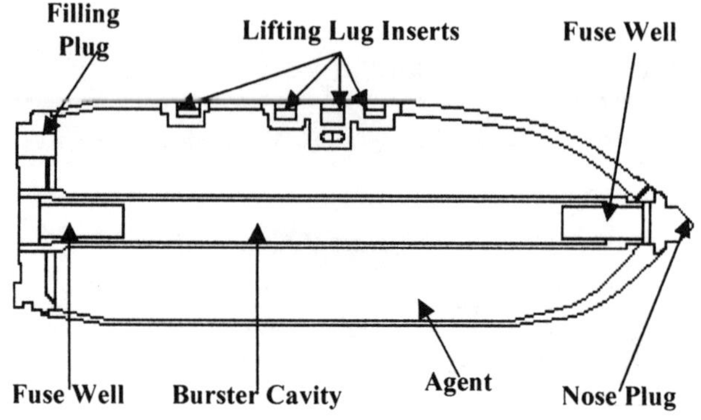

MC-1—750-lb. Aerial Bomb

CHARACTERISTICS

Length:	50 inches
Diameter:	16 inches
Agent:	GB
Agent Weight:	220 pounds
Total Weight:	725 pounds

MK-94—500-lb. Aerial Bomb

CHARACTERISTICS

Length:	60 inches
Diameter:	11 inches
Agent:	GB
Agent Weight:	108 pounds
Total Weight:	441 pounds

MK-116—Weteye Aerial Bomb

CHARACTERISTICS

Length:	86 inches
Diameter:	14 inches
Agent:	GB
Agent Weight:	347 pounds
Total Weight:	525 pounds

MISCELLANEOUS

TMU-28/B Spray Tank

See Figure 3.15.

CHARACTERISTICS

Length:	185 inches
Diameter:	22.5 inches
Agent:	VX
Agent Weight:	1,356 pounds
Total Weight:	1,935 pounds

Figure 3.15
Cutaway View of Chemical Agent Spray Tank

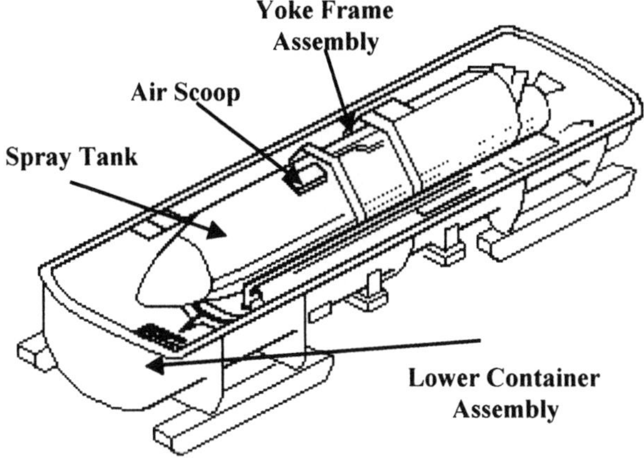

Ton Container

See Figure 3.16.

CHARACTERISTICS

Length:	81.5 inches			
Diameter:	30.1 inches			
Agent:	HD, HT, L	GB	VX	
Total Weight:	3,100	2,900	3,000	pounds
Agent Weight:	1,700	1,500	1,600	pounds

Figure 3.16
Cutaway View of a Ton Container

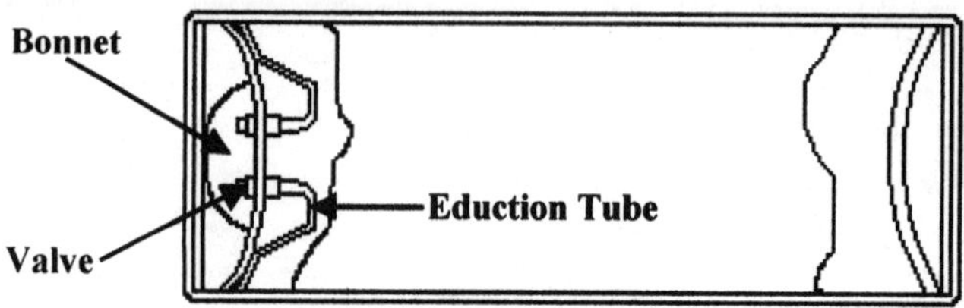

4

Protection and Decontamination

CIVILIAN CHEMICAL PROTECTION LEVELS

Selection of the appropriate personal protective equipment (PPE) is a complex process that should take into consideration a variety of factors. Key factors involved in this process are identification of the hazards or suspected hazards; the routes of potential hazards (inhalation, skin absorption, ingestion, and eye or skin contact); and the performance of the PPE materials in providing a barrier to these hazards. The amount of protection provided by PPE is material hazard-specific. That is, protective equipment materials will protect well against some hazardous substances and poorly, or not at all, against others. In many instances, protective equipment materials cannot be found that will provide continuous protection from the particular hazardous substances. In these cases the breakthrough time of the protective material should exceed the work durations.

Other factors in this selection process to be considered are matching the PPE to the employee's work requirements and task-specific conditions. The durability of PPE materials, such as tear strength and seam strength, should be considered in relation to the employee's tasks. The effects of PPE in relation to heat stress and task duration are a factor in selecting and using PPE. In some cases layers of PPE may be necessary to provide sufficient protection or to protect expensive PPE inner garments, suits, or equipment.

The more that is known about the hazards at the site, the easier the job of PPE selection becomes. As more information about the hazards and conditions at the site becomes available, the site supervisor can make decisions to upgrade or downgrade the level of PPE protection to match the tasks at hand.

The following are guidelines to begin the selection of the appropriate PPE. As noted earlier, the site information may suggest the use of combinations of PPE selected from the different protection levels (i.e., A, B, C, or D) as being more suitable to the hazards of the work. It should be cautioned that the following does not fully address the performance of the specific PPE material in relation to the specific hazards at the job site and that PPE selection, evaluation, and reselection are an ongoing process until sufficient information about the hazards and PPE performance is obtained.

- **Level A** - Level A protection should be used when the hazardous substance has been identified and requires the highest level of protection for skin, eyes, and the respiratory system based on either the measured (or potential for) high concentration of atmospheric vapors, gases, or particulates; or when the site operations and work functions involve a high potential for splash, immersion, or exposure to unexpected vapors, gases, or particulates of materials that are harmful to skin or capable of being absorbed through the skin. Substances with a high degree of hazard to the skin are known or suspected to be present, and skin contact is possible or when operations are being conducted in confined, poorly ventilated areas, and the absence of conditions requiring Level A have not yet been determined.
  (a) Positive-pressure, full-facepiece, self-contained breathing apparatus (SCBA) or positive pressure-supplied air respirator with escape SCBA, approved by the National Institute for Occupational Safety and Health (NIOSH).
  (b) Totally encapsulating chemical protective suit.
  (c) Coveralls (optional).
  (d) Long underwear (optional).
  (e) Gloves, outer, chemical-resistant.
  (f) Gloves, inner, chemical-resistant.
  (g) Boots, chemical-resistant, steel toe and shank.
  (h) Hard hat (under suit) (optional).
  (i) Disposable protective suit, gloves, and boots (depending on suit construction, may be worn over totally encapsulating suit).

- **Level B** - Level B protection should be used when the type and atmospheric concentration of substances have been identified and require a high level of respiratory protection, but less skin protection, and when the atmosphere contains less than 19.5% oxygen or when the presence of incompletely identified vapors or gases is indicated by a direct-reading organic vapor detection instrument, but vapors and gases are not suspected of containing high levels of chemicals harmful to skin or capable of being absorbed through the skin.

(a) Positive-pressure, full-facepiece SCBA or positive pressure supplied air respirator with escape SCBA (NIOSH-approved).
(b) Hooded, chemical-resistant clothing (overalls and long-sleeved jacket; coveralls; one- or two-piece chemical splash suit; disposable chemical-resistant overalls).
(c) Coveralls (optional).
(d) Gloves, outer, chemical-resistant.
(e) Gloves, inner, chemical-resistant.
(f) Boots, outer, chemical-resistant steel toe and shank.
(g) Bootcovers, outer, chemical-resistant (disposable).
(h) Hard hat (optional).
(i) Face shield (optional).

- **Level C** - Level C protection should be used when the atmospheric contaminants, liquid splashes, or other direct contact will not adversely affect or be absorbed through any exposed skin. The types of air contaminants have been identified, concentrations have been measured, and an air-purifying respirator is available that can remove the contaminants, and all criteria for the use of air-purifying respirators are met.
(a) Full face or half mask, air-purifying respirators (NIOSH-approved).
(b) Hooded, chemical-resistant clothing (overalls; two-piece chemical splash suit; disposable, chemical-resistant overalls).
(c) Coveralls (optional).
(d) Gloves, outer, chemical-resistant.
(e) Gloves, inner, chemical-resistant.
(f) Boots (outer), chemical-resistant steel toe and shank (optional).
(g) Bootcovers, outer, chemical-resistant (disposable—optional).
(h) Hard hat (optional).
(i) Escape mask (optional).
(j) Face shield (optional).

- **Level D** - Level D protection should be used when the atmosphere contains no known hazard; and work functions preclude splashes, immersion, or the potential for unexpected inhalation of, or contact with, hazardous levels of any chemicals.
(a) Coveralls.
(b) Gloves.
(c) Boots/shoes, chemical-resistant steel toe and shank.
(d) Boots, outer, chemical-resistant (disposable—optional).
(e) Safety glasses or chemical splash goggles.
(f) Hard hat (optional).
(g) Escape mask (optional).
(h) Face shield (optional).

The Occupational Safety and Health Administration (OSHA) requires Level A protection for workers in environments known to be immediately dangerous to life and health (i.e., where escape will be impaired or irreversible harm will occur within 30 minutes) and specifies Level B as the minimum protection for workers in danger of exposure to unknown chemical hazards. The NIOSH and the Mine Safety and Health Administration (MSHA) designate performance characteristics for respirators and provide approval for all commercially available respirators. Chemical-protective clothing is not subject to performance standards established by any government agency, but the American Society for Testing and Materials (ASTM), an independent organization, has developed methods for testing the permeability of protective clothing materials against a battery of liquids and gases. The National Fire Protection Association (NFPA) has incorporated the ASTM test battery into the currently accepted standards for protective suits for hazardous chemical emergencies. Although a basic rule in selecting personal protective equipment (PPE) is that the equipment be matched to the hazard, none of the ASTM permeability tests employ military nerve agents or vesicants. However, the NFPA is currently in the process of developing testing standards that will address the threat of nerve agents, cyanides, and vesicants.

CIVILIAN DECONTAMINATION PROCEDURES

Fire departments and hazardous material teams have traditionally described the decontamination processes with two terms—"technical decon" and "medical decon" or "patient decon." "Technical decon" is the process used to clean vehicles and personal protective equipment (PPE), and "medical decon" or "patient decon" is the process of cleaning injured or exposed individuals.

Technical Decontamination

Technical decontamination is most commonly performed using a sequential, nine-step process originally developed by Noll and Hildebrand (1994)[1]. The steps are as follows:

HOT ZONE

1	Contaminated tools and equipment drop onto a plastic sheet.
2	Contaminated trash drop.

WARM ZONE

3	Primary garment wash/rinse (boots, gloves, suit, SCBA, and mask.)
4	Primary garment removal.
5	Secondary garment wash/rinse (decon inner garment and gloves).
6	Face piece removal/drop (can be combined with stations 7 and 8).

7	Boot drop.
8	Inner glove removal.
	COLD ZONE
9	Shower and clothing change.

This process is well known and extensively utilized by the public safety community. Cleaning is done using water in conjunction with one of four cleaning solutions (solutions known as A, B, C, D), depending on the type of contaminant. Solution "A" contains 5% sodium bicarbonate and 5% trisodium phosphate and is used for inorganic acids, acidic caustic wastes, solvents and organic compounds, plastic wastes, polychlorinated biphenyls (PCBs), and biologic contamination. Solution "B" is a concentrated solution of sodium hypochlorite. A 10% solution is used for radioactive materials, pesticides, chlorinated phenols, dioxin, PCBs, cyanide, ammonia, inorganic wastes, organic wastes, and biologic contamination. Solution "C" is a rinse solution of 5% trisodium phosphate. It is used for solvents and organic compounds, PCBs, and polybrominated biphenyls (PBB), and oily wastes not suspected to be contaminated with pesticides. Solution "D" is dilute hydrochloric acid. It is used for inorganic bases, alkalis, and alkali caustic wastes.

Once the decon process is completed, the equipment is most often returned to service, unless the item(s) cannot be completely decontaminated (as determined by using available detection devices). However, current research does not provide an answer to the question, How clean is clean? Some communities will depend on disposable equipment as an alternative to trying to assure that each item has been thoroughly decontaminated. Other communities may not be able to afford the replacement cost and depend on using available technology or best guess to determine when these items are "clean." It will be important for emergency responders to know when complete technical decontamination has been achieved, if the equipment is to be reused. It is vital when personal protective clothing or equipment is involved.

Patient Decontamination

Patient decontamination, which Hazmat teams have to undertake much less often than technical decon, is to be performed when the contaminant poses a further risk to the patient or a secondary risk to response personnel. Fire and Emergency Medical Services (EMS) publications frequently describe how patient decontamination can be done, but few of the recommendations are based on empirical research. Because little scientific documentation exists for when and how patient decontamination should be performed expeditiously and costeffectively, prehospital and hospital providers are left to do what they think is right, rather than what has been proven to work best. Generally, the process involves three stages: gross, secondary, and definitive decontamination.

- Gross Decon
    1. Evacuate the patient(s) from the high-risk area.
    2. Remove the patient's clothing.
    3. Perform a one-minute, quick, head-to-toe rinse with water.

- Secondary Decon
    1. Perform a quick, full-body rinse with water.
    2. Wash rapidly with cleaning solution from head to toe.
    3. Rinse with water from head to toe.

- Definitive Decon
    1. Perform thorough head-to-toe wash until "clean".
    2. Rinse with water thoroughly.
    3. Towel off and have person put on clean clothes.

As noted, among the first steps in the decontamination process are the removal and disposal of clothing. It has been estimated that 70 to 80% of contamination will be removed with the patient's clothes. Little scientific data exist to support this assertion, however. The ideal skin decontaminant would remove and neutralize a wide range of hazardous chemicals, and be cheap, readily available, rapid-acting, and safe. For most civilian applications, water has been the choice; the technical decontaminant solutions cannot be safely used to clean the skin or mucous membranes. The armed forces have assessed a wide variety of skin decontaminants, including flour, Fuller's earth, and absorbent ion-exchange resin for environments where water is not available. A fresh solution of 0.5% sodium hypochlorite appears to be the state-of-the-art liquid decontaminating agent for personnel contaminated with chemical or biological agents (Chemical Casualty Care Office, 1995)[2]. The half-life of sarin in undiluted household bleach, which is 5.0% sodium hypochlorite and generally too harsh for use on skin, is on the order of three seconds.

Civilian Hazmat teams generally have basic decontamination plans in place, though proficiency may vary widely. Very few, if any, teams are manned, equipped, or trained for mass decontamination, however. Again, water is the principal decontamination solution, with soap recommended for oily or otherwise adherent chemicals. Some teams suggest that initial mass decontamination be accomplished by fire hose (operated at reduced pressure), which has the advantage of being possible even before the Hazmat team arrives on the scene. Shower systems with provisions for capturing contaminated runoff are commercially available and may provide some measure of privacy in incidents involving only a handful of victims (they generally accommodate only one person at a time). However, the availability of trained personnel in appropriate personal protective clothing is likely to be a limiting factor, even when larger shower units or multiple smaller ones are available. The Chemical

Biological Incident Response Force (CBIRF) have much larger shower units, capable of decontaminating dozens to hundreds of victims with sodium hypochlorite solution, and are staffed at much higher levels than local Hazmat teams. However, neither will be immediately available unless predeployed (e.g., as was done at the Atlanta Olympics and State of the Union Address). Harsh weather, intrusive media, and the willingness of ambulatory patients to disrobe in less than private surroundings will also affect the conduct of field decontamination. Where there are very large numbers in need of decontamination, crowd control measures will be necessary to keep panicky or merely impatient victims at the scene long enough to complete decontamination.

The degree to which a patient is decontaminated in the prehospital setting depends on the decon plan, available resources, the weather, and patient volume. At minimum, every patient presenting a risk of secondary contamination risk should receive gross decon before departing for the hospital. These patients should be transported to a hospital (by properly protected Emergency Medical Technicians and paramedics). The receiving hospital should be equipped and staffed to perform secondary and definitive decon, if not already done in the field.

Patients requiring additional medical attention, such as attention to the ABCs (airway, breathing, and circulation), antidotes, or other emergency treatment may receive that care during or after the decontamination process depending on the severity of the agents' effects and the ability of the decon team and available medical personnel to render that care. Nonambulatory patients pose much more of a decontamination and treatment burden than ambulatory patients, because most portable decontamination chambers require a person to stand. Decontamination and treatment planning must also address how to deal with the pediatric patient and the elderly.

Although hospitals are required by the Joint Commission on Accreditation of Healthcare Organizations (JCAHO) to be prepared to respond to disasters, including hazardous material accidents, few have undertaken realistic planning and preparation. Some hospitals have decontamination facilities; however, very few have outdoor facilities or an easy way of expanding their decontamination operations in a mass-casualty event. Often their initial response to an incident will be to contact the local fire department or Hazmat team for assistance. This will not be a viable solution if the incident is large or nearby. Unannounced ambulance or walk-in patients who are contaminated may create havoc and harm before "outside" help arrives to address the situation or internal resources can be organized to respond. If assistance from the local public safety agency is not available, the hospital is left to fend for itself, and, if unprepared, the response is likely to place the patient, staff, and facility at great risk. There is little financial incentive for a hospital to be prepared for a "once in a lifetime" event, and proper equipment and training may be perceived as too expensive under the circumstances. Generally, hospitals that are prepared are usually capable of handling only a few patients an hour. What happens when a large number of patients begin to arrive? Currently, the medical literature does not contain sufficient research findings to assist hospitals with cost-effective Hazmat or terrorist response planning. The Agency for Toxic Substances and Disease Registry recently released a series of guidelines to help local emergency departments, communities, and other policymakers develop their own response plan for hazardous materials incidents, and the Centers for Disease Control (CDC) and Prevention's Planning Guidance for the Chemical Stockpile Emergency Preparedness Program (CSEPP) provide recommendations for civilian communities near chemical weapons depots. Although helpful, the outlines are very generic, do not address how to actually perform mass decon, and do not contain information on many of the agents that are likely to be seen in a terrorist incident. Since planning is left to the local jurisdictions, the success of any national initiative is dependent upon cooperation at the local level.

Aside from the issues related to effective decontamination procedures, training of emergency department personnel must also be considered. There are few courses that emergency department personnel may attend to improve their level of preparation for mass decontamination.

MILITARY CHEMICAL PROTECTION LEVELS

The level of protection required will be determined by the hazard analyses for each operation and must be specified in the standard operating procedures manual. Levels may be modified if a particular operation requires a level of protection other than the one specified. For example, the protective mask may be worn with levels E or F. The various levels of protection are discussed next.

- **Level A**—will be worn in areas below immediate danger to life and health (IDLH) and/or at/above 0.003 mg/m^3 for mustard and lewisite environments when liquid agent is present. For these situations, the cuffs of the sleeves and legs of the M3 Toxicological Agent Protective (TAP) suit may be taped to the gloves and boots to reduce the amount of outside air drawn into the suit.
  (a) Suit coveralls, TAP (M3).
  (b) Hood, TAP (M3, M40 SP).
  (c) Boots, butyl, safety toe, TAP (M2A1).
  (d) Gloves, butyl, TAP (M3, M4, glove set). GB/VX surgical or other equivalent, nonstandard gloves will be worn underneath for protection when doffing TAP clothing. Mustard surgical or other equivalent nonstandard gloves are optional. Surgical gloves will not be worn in operations where exposed explosives or propellants are present or where a hazard analysis indicates electrostatic initiation is possible.

(e) Innerwear, GB/VX coveralls, fatigues, or equivalent government-issued clothing (with drawers and undershirt) and socks. Alternative—long underwear and socks. Mustard- and lewisite-impregnated gloves, impregnated socks, impregnated long underwear, or impregnated protective liner to include shirt and trousers (only during intrusive operations and/or operations without real-time monitoring), or the chemical protective undergarment (CPU) with socks and gloves. Coveralls, fatigues, equivalent government-issued clothing or unimpregnated underwear may be worn in addition.

(f) Mask. Mask-worn (M9 and M40 series).

- **Alternate Level A**—will be worn in IDLH and/or 0.003 mg/m^3 for mustard and lewisite environments. In proximity to spilled agent in an area of known liquid contamination and whenever realtime monitoring with alarm capabilities is not available and when in areas of potential, but unknown, airborne contamination.

- **Level A—DPE.** The demilitarization protective ensemble (DPE), 20 and 30 mil. The DPE is a totally encapsulating, chemical-protective suit that operates at a positive pressure to assure total protection against inward leaks. The DPE is an air-supplied ensemble with a 10-minute emergency internal breathing system. The suit is designed to be worn in IDLH and/or 0.003 mg/m3 for mustard and lewisite environments. DPE is a onetime-use-only suit.

- **Level A—TAPES.** The toxicological agent-protective ensemble, self-contained, one-hour (TAPES). The TAPES is a totally encapsulating, positive-pressure air pack suit with an integrated cooling system designed for a one-hour mission in IDLH and/or 0.003 mg/m3 for mustard and lewisite environments. TAPES is approved for use with G series, VX, L, and H series agents. Wearing of the 20-mil TAPES in a mustard environment is limited to one hour at 80°F or less and no more than 45 minutes in temperatures between 80 and 90°F.The 20-mil TAPES is not authorized for use in mustard environments at temperatures exceeding 90°F.

- **Level A—Modified.** M3 suit with M30 hood and SCBA, pressure demand (Modified Level A). This ensemble is not a positive-pressure system. The modified M3 TAP utilizes a pressure demand, self-contained breathing apparatus and full-face respirator in a modified M30 hood and is authorized for use in IDLH and/or 0.003 mg/m^3 for lewisite and mustard environments.

- **Level A—STEPO-I.** The self-contained toxicological environmental protective outfit for use in immediate danger to life and health (IDLH) and/or 0.003 mg/m^3 for mustard and lewisite environments. It provides total encapsulation for the user. The suit is provided with an air line of the same butyl rubber material as the M3 TAP ensemble. Impregnated undergarments are not required for operations in a mustard environment.

- **Level B**—will be worn when contact with suspect item is required and when performing operations that may result in release of agent vapors within the work area but there is no contact with liquid agent anticipated, and no liquid agent is present. May be worn by personnel performing first-entry monitoring of outdoor storage areas. Is required for loading and charging the M12 decontaminating apparatus with Super Tropical Bleach (STB) or High Test Hypochlorite (HTH) in an atmosphere free of chemical agent contamination.
  (a) Apron TAP (M2); extending below top of boots.
  (b) Innerwear GB/VX coveralls, fatigues, or equivalent government-issued clothing (with drawers and undershirt) and socks. Mustard-impregnated gloves; impregnated socks; and impregnated protective liner to include shirt and trousers (only during intrusive operations and/or operations without real-time monitoring) or the CPU with socks and gloves. Coveralls, fatigues, equivalent government-issued clothing, or unimpregnated underwear may be worn in addition.
  (c) Hood TAP; M3 for M9 mask, M3A1 for M40 mask or M6A2 for M17 mask.
  (d) Boots butyl, safety toe, TAP (M2A1).
  (e) Gloves butyl, TAP (M3, M4, glove set). GB/VX-surgical or other equivalent nonstandard gloves will be worn underneath for protection when doffing TAP clothing. Mustard-surgical or other equivalent nonstandard gloves are optional. Surgical gloves will not be worn in operations where exposed explosives or propellants are present or where a hazard analysis indicates electrostatic initiation is possible.
  (f) Mask worn (M9-, M17- or M40-series).

- **Level C**—will be worn by personnel who must be in agent areas where handling or contact with agent-filled items is involved and if real-time monitoring to IDLH and/or 0.003 mg/m^3 for mustard and lewisite level is being performed.
  (a) Boots butyl, safety toe, TAP (M2A1).
  (b) Gloves butyl, (M3, M4, glove set).

(c) Apron TAP (M2), extending below top of boots. Required only if hazard analysis determines that bodily contact with agent-filled items may occur.
(d) Clothing unimpregnated coveralls or fatigues, or equivalent government-issued clothing, socks, drawers, undershirt.
(e) Mask worn (M9-, M17- or M40-series).

- **Level D**—will be worn by personnel in clean areas where handling or contact with agent filled items is involved provided that real-time, low-level monitoring with alarm is being performed at or below the AEL, with negative results.
  (a) Boots butyl, safety toe, TAP (M2A1).
  (b) Gloves butyl, (M3, M4, glove set).
  (c) Apron TAP (M2); extending below top of boots. Required only if hazards analysis determines that bodily contact with agent-filled items may occur.
  (d) Clothing unimpregnated coveralls, fatigues, or equivalent government-issued clothing, socks, drawers, undershirt.
  (e) Mask slung position (M9-, M17- or M40-series).

- **Level E**—will be worn by operating personnel who may be observing or supervising the operations and who would not likely contact an item or would be exposed to agent only in the event of an accident. Laboratory personnel will use this level of protection in conjunction with approved gloves as required. A laboratory coat may be substituted for the coveralls and masks may be readily available instead of in the slung position.
  (a) Clothing unimpregnated coveralls, fatigues, or equivlent government-issued clothing, socks, drawers, undershirt.
  (b) Mask slung position (M9-, M17- or M40-series). For laboratories, the mask may be readily available at the work site instead of in a slung position.
  (c) In laboratories, a lab coat may be substituted for coveralls, fatigues, or equivalent government-issued clothing.
  (d) Gloves will be worn when the hazard analysis determines handling of agent-filled containers may occur.
  (e) Safety shoes if job hazard analysis determines the necessity.

- **Level F**—is limited to casual or transient personnel who may be required to visit clean storage or operating areas.
  (a) Street clothing.
  (b) Mask slung position (M9-, M17- or M40-series).

MISSION ORIENTED PROTECTIVE POSTURE (MOPP)

All military personnel need to be familiar with standard Mission Oriented Protective Posture or MOPP levels. MOPP is the military version of protection against chemcial warfare. Knowing these levels will aid the military in making rapid and educated decisions regarding the level of MOPP to be worn by soldiers. Standardized MOPP levels allow soldiers to increase or decrease levels of protection.

The commander's or leader's directive also can include, based on the threat, the percentage of soldiers who will mask: for example, MOPP 1, 50% masked. The system is flexible, and subordinate leaders can modify their units' MOPP level to meet mission needs.

The following standardized protective postures assume that personnel are also carrying their individual decontamination kit (M258A1 or M291), M8/M9 detector paper, Nerve Agent Antidote Kit (NAAK), and their protective mask, unless the threat assessment indicates a zero% probability of chemical agents. See Table 4.1.

Table 4.1
MOPP Levels

MOPP Equipment	MOPP Levels						
	MOPP Ready	MOPP 0	MOPP 1	MOPP 2	MOPP 3	MOPP 4	Mask Only
Mask	Carried	Carried	Carried	Carried	Worn	Worn	Worn
BDO	Ready	Available	Worn	Worn	Worn	Worn	
Overboot	Ready	Available	Available	Worn	Worn	Worn	
Gloves	Ready	Available	Available	Available	Available	Worn	
Helmet	Ready	Available	Available	Worn	Worn	Worn	

- **MOPP Ready**—Soldiers carry their protective masks. The soldier's MOPP gear is labeled and stored in the rear and is ready to be brought forward to the soldier when needed. Bringing it forward should not exceed two hours. Units in MOPP Ready are highly vulnerable to persistent agent attacks and will automatically upgrade to MOPP Zero when they determine, or are notified, that chemical weapons have been used or that the threat for use of chemical weapons has risen. When a unit is at MOPP Ready, soldiers will have field-expedient items identified for use.

- **MOPP Zero**—Soldiers carry their protective masks. The standard Battle Dress Overgarment (BDO) and other equipment making up the soldier's

MOPP gear are readily available. To be considered readily available, equipment must be either carried by each soldier or stored within arm's reach of the soldier, for example, within the work area, vehicle, or fighting position. Units in MOPP 0 are highly vulnerable to persistent agent attacks and will automatically upgrade to MOPP 1 when they determine, or are notified, that persistent chemical weapons have been used or that the threat for use of chemical weapons has risen.

- **MOPP 1**—When directed to MOPP 1, soldiers immediately don the Battle Dress Overgarment (BDO). In hot weather, the overgarment jacket can be unbuttoned, and the BDO can be worn directly over underwear. M9 or M8 chemical detection paper is attached to the overgarment. MOPP 1 provides a great deal of protection against persistent agents. This level is automatically assumed when chemical agents have been employed in an area of operations or when directed by higher commands.

- **MOPP 2**—Soldiers put on their Chemical Protective Footwear Covers (CPFCs), Green Vinyl Overboots (GVOS), or a field-expedient item (e.g., vapor-barrier boots), and the protective helmet cover is worn. As with MOPP 1, the overgarment jacket may be left unbuttoned, but trousers remain closed.

- **MOPP 3**—Soldiers wear the protective mask and hood. Again, flexibility is built into the system to allow soldiers relief at MOPP 3. Particularly in hot weather, soldiers can open the overgarment jacket and roll the protective mask hood for ventilation, but trousers remain closed.

- **MOPP 4**—Soldiers will completely encapsulate themselves by closing their overgarments, rolling down and adjusting the mask hood, and putting on rubber gloves with cotton liners. MOPP 4 provides the highest degree of chemical protection but also has the most negative impact on an individual's performance.

- **Mask Only**—The mask is worn. The Mask Only command is given in these situations: when riot control agents are being employed, and no chemical/biological threat exists. Mask Only is not an appropriate command when blister or persistent nerve agents are present.

MILITARY DECONTAMINATION PROCEDURES

Whenever soldiers are unable to avoid contamination and have to use protective measures, decon is necessary to allow them to remove their protective gear and resume normal operations. Weathering is the most desirable means of decon; however, time and operational needs may not permit that option.

This section describes when, where, and how much to decon. Protective clothing (Mission Oriented Protective Posture [MOPP] gear), protective equipment, and Collective Protective Shelters (CPSs) offer only a temporary solution. Decon is the removal, destruction, or naturalization of contamination. If you become contaminated, some decon must occur as soon as possible.

The decision to decon is a risk assessment and is made within the context of the mission, enemy, terrain, troops, time available, and civilian considerations and the resources available. Decon must be considered if the contamination levels exceed negligible risk levels:

> Chemical contamination causing mild incapacitation in 5 percent or less of unprotected soldiers operating for 12 continuous hours within 1 meter of contamination. For the chemical agent monitor (CAM), this equates to a one-bar reading at a distance of 1 inch from the surface.

MOPP gear exchange provides excellent protection against field concentrations of agents;, however, wearing the gear causes performance degradation. Decon is performed to restore the normal operating tempo, but the logistical support that is required to keep soldiers in MOPP gear impacts operations. Therefore, decon should be conducted as soon as practical. Table 4.2 provides comparison data for decon levels/techniques.

Table 4.2
Comparison Data for Decon Levels/Techniques

Levels	Techniques[1]	Best Start Time	Performed by
Immediate	Skin decon Personal wipedown Operator's spray down	Before 1 minute Within 15 minutes	Individual Individual or crew
Operational	MOPP gear exchange[2] Vehicle wash-down[3]	Within 6 hours	Unit Decon platoon or crew
Thorough	Detailed Equipment Decon Detailed Troop Decon	When mission allows reconstitution	Decon platoon Unit

Notes:
1. The techniques become less effective the longer they are delayed.
2. Performance degradation and risk assessment must be considered when exceeding 6 hours.
3. Vehicle wash-down is most effective if started within 1 hour.

The three levels of decontamination (decon) operations employed by the military are immediate, operational, and thorough.

Immediate Decon

Once a soldier is aware of chemical contamination on his bare skin, he initiates immediate decon techniques, without command, by using his personal Skin Decon Kit (SDK). He decontaminates his hood, mask, gloves, and weapon using the Individual Equipment Decon Kit (IEDK) or an additional SDK.

There are three immediate techniques: skin decon, personnel wipe-down, and operator's spray-down.

Skin Decon

Start the skin decon techniques within one minute of becoming contaminated. Some toxic chemical agents, especially nerve agents, kill in minutes.

Use the SDKs within one minute of contamination. Instructions for use are listed on the outside of the kit itself and on the individual packet within the kit.

If an SDK is not available, chemical contamination may be pinch-blotted from the skin with a cloth and flushed with water from a canteen. Soap, if available, can also be used to wash the agent from the skin. Washing with soap and water (or hot water) is the next best method for toxic agent decon if SDKs are not available, but this method is not as effective as using the decon kits.

Washing with soap and water removes nearly all biological agents from the skin. A 0.5% chlorine (calcium hypochlorite [high-test hypochlorite HTH] or household bleach) solution is an effective biological decontaminant. See later in chapter for details on how to make this solution.

Personal Wipe-Down

The personal wipe-down techniques are most effective when done within 15 minutes of being contaminated. The CAM and/or M8/M9 detector paper is used to detect and monitor equipment.

Wipe down your mask, hood, gloves, and other essential gear. Do not attempt to remove chemical contamination from your protective overgarment unless there are obvious clumps of the agent. In this case, scrape off the material. Brush off frozen chemical agent contamination.

Decon individual equipment using the IEDKs. Wearing your Kevlar helmet protective cover will prevent or reduce the adsorption of any liquid chemical agent. Washing with soap and water and bleach solutions is partially effective.

Operator's Spray Down

Decon other mission-essential portions of your equipment before continuing your mission. The CAM and/or M8/M9 detector paper is used to determine what surfaces require decon.

Operator's spray-down is most effective when done within 15 minutes of contamination.

Decon those surfaces that you must touch on the exterior of the vehicle or equipment that you must use to do your job with the onboard portable decon apparatus, such as the M11 or M13 (see Chapter 5). The IEDK may be used on equipment that Decon Solution 2 (DS2) may cause damage to by corrosive action.

Scrub the DS2 into the exterior surface with brushes. Wait 30 minutes and then wash off. If a decon apparatus is not available, use the field-expedient resources that are available to apply DS2 or Super Tropical Bleach (STB) from bulk containers.

Operational Decontamination

There are two operational decon tehniques: MOPP gear exchange and vehicle wash-down.

A MOPP gear exchange should be performed within six hours of being contaminated when thorough decon cannot be done. Soldiers will continue to wear MOPP gear, and the operating tempo will be reduced.

Vehicle wash-down should be performed within six hours of being contaminated when the mission does not permit a thorough decon. This process removes gross contamination and limits its spread.

MOPP Gear Exchange

Buddy Team Method

This method uses pairs of soldiers under the supervision of their squad/ team leader to conduct the buddy team MOPP ear exchange. Detailed, step-by-step procedures for this method follow.

Step 1—Decon Gear

Removes gross contamination from individual gear (weapons, helmet, load-bearing equipment, and mask carrier).

The soldier mixes three parts earth to two parts STB. The soldier removes and discards the chemical protective helmet cover if worn. He brushes or rubs STB onto his individual gear (helmet and mask carrier) and the hose of the M42 or M43 mask if worn. He gently shakes off any excess STB and sets aside his gear on an uncontaminated surface.

Step 2—Prepare to Decon

Facilitates later removal of overgarment trousers and overboots.

Buddy #1 unfastens the shoulder straps on Buddy #2's hood and pulls them over his shoulder and reattaches them to the Velcro fasteners. He loosens the drawcord on Buddy #2's hood. He removes the M9 detector paper from Buddy #2's overgarment. He unties the drawcords on the trouser legs of Buddy #2's overgarment. He unzips Buddy #2's trouser legs and rolls a cuff in each trouser leg, ensuring that the cuffs do not come above the tops of his overboots. He unfastens or cuts the fasteners on Buddy #2's overboots. A soldier can do this step by himself or with the help of his buddy. When wearing overboots, unsnap both quick releases on the overboots. The M40 voice amplifier (M7) and the M42A2 detachable microphone cannot be decontaminated and will be disposed of as contaminated waste; however, ensure that these items are contaminated before disposing of them.

Step 3—Decon Mask and Hood

Removes gross contamination.

Buddy #1 uses an IEDK to wipe Buddy #2's eye-lens outserts from the top down. Do not press so hard that you break Buddy #2's facemask seal. He then wipes the rest of Buddy #2's hood from the top of the head to the bottom of the hood. After he has finished wiping Buddy #2's mask, he must wipe his own gloves in preparation for rolling Buddy #2's hood. He starts from the rear and rolls Buddy #2's hood, using two inch tucks, until it reaches the center of his head. He rolls the front of Buddy #2's hood tightly under the outlet valve and filter. He ensures that the hood is off Buddy #2's garment.

Step 4—Remove Overgarments and Overboots

Limits the spread of agents and helps prevent agents from penetrating through to the undergarments or the skin.

Buddy #1 grasps Buddy #2's overgarment jacket, unsnaps the snaps individually, and unties the drawcord at the bottom of the jacket. He unfastens the Velcro at the wrist of Buddy #2's jacket and then refastens it. He unfastens the Velcro closure over the zippered front of Buddy #2's jacket and unzips the jacket. He grasps Buddy #2's jacket at the shoulders and instructs him to make a fist. He then pulls Buddy #2's jacket down and away from him, ensuring that the black part of the jacket is not touched. He lays Buddy #2's overgarment jacket on the ground, black side up. (It will be used to stand on later.) He carefully unfastens and unzips Buddy #2's trousers. Do not loosen Buddy #2's waist tabs.

He instructs Buddy #2 to loosen his overboots by alternately stepping on each heel and pulling up on his foot. He grasps Buddy #2's trousers and pulls them down to his knees. He instructs Buddy #2 to walk out of his trousers/overboots simultaneously and step onto the black side of the jacket. Buddy #2 should step onto the jacket wearing his mask, Battle Dress Uniform (BDU), combat boots, and gloves.

Step 5—Remove Gloves

The soldier holds the fingertips of his gloves and partially slides his hand out. When the fingers of both hands are free, he holds his arms away from his body and lets the gloves drop.

Step 6—Put on Overgarment

Buddy #1 opens the package containing the new overgarment without touching the inside of the package. Buddy #2 pulls out the overgarment without touching the outside of the package. He puts on the overgarment and fastens it, leaving the trouser legs open. Do not reverse roles. Only Buddy #2 will put on the clean overgarment at this time.

Step 7—Put on Overboots and Gloves

Buddy #1 opens the package of clean overboots without touching the inside of the package. Buddy #2 removes the overboots from the package without touching the outside of the package, puts them on, and fastens his trouser legs. Buddy #1 opens the package of clean gloves without touching the inside of the package. Buddy #2 removes the gloves from the package without touching the outside of the package and puts them on. Buddy #2 puts on the M9 detector paper. Do not reverse roles. Only Buddy #2 will put on the clean overboots and gloves at this time.

Step 8—Secure Hood

Buddy #1 uses an IEDK to wipe Buddy #2's gloves. He unrolls Buddy #2's hood and attaches the straps and tightens the neck cord. Buddy #1 and Buddy #2 reverse roles and repeat steps 2 through 8.

Step 9—Secure Gear

The soldier secures his individual gear and puts it back on. He puts on a new chemical protective helmet cover and moves to the Assembly Area (AA). He uses the buddy system to check the fit of all secured gear.

Triple Buddy Team Method

This method is used by soldiers equipped with the M40A1, M42, or M43 mask with the quick-doff hood. A third soldier is needed to hold the filter canister and hose to prevent the transfer of contamination.

Step 1—Decon Gear

Removes gross contamination from individual gear (weapons, helmet, load-bearing equipment, and mask carrier).

The soldier mixes three parts earth to two parts STB. The soldier removes and discards the chemical protective helmet cover if worn. He brushes or rubs STB onto his individual gear (helmet and mask carrier) and the hose of the M42 or M43 mask, if worn. He gently shakes off any excess STB and sets aside his gear on an uncontaminated surface.

Step 2—Prepare to Decon

Facilitates later removal of overgarment trousers and overboots.

Buddy #1 unfastens the shoulder straps on Buddy #2's hood and pulls them over his shoulder and reattaches them to the Velcro fastener. He loosens the drawcord on Buddy #2's hood and ties off the microphone cord to the hose of his mask. He removes the M9 detector paper from Buddy #2's overgarment. He unzips Buddy #2's trouser legs and rolls a cuff in each trouser leg, ensuring that the cuffs do not come above the tops of his overboots. He unfastens or cuts the fasteners on Buddy #2's overboots. A soldier can do this step by himself or with the help of his buddy.

Step 3—Decon Mask and Hood

Removes gross contamination.

Buddy #1 uses an IEDK to wipe Buddy #2's eye-lens outserts from the top down. Do not press so hard that you break Buddy #2's facemask seal. He then wipes the rest of Buddy #2's hood from the top of the head to the bottom of the hood. After he has finished wiping Buddy #2's mask, he must wipe his own gloves in preparation for rolling Buddy #2's hood. He starts from the rear and rolls Buddy #2's hood, using two inch tucks, until it reaches the center of his head. He rolls the front of Buddy #2's hood tightly under the outlet valve and filter. He ensures that the hood is off of Buddy #2's garment.

Step 4—Remove Overgarments and Overboots

Limits the spread of agents and helps prevent agents from penetrating through to the undergarments or the skin.

Buddy #1 grasps Buddy #2's outside overgarment jacket, unsnaps the snaps individually, and unties the drawcord at the bottom of the jacket. He unfastens the Velcro at the wrist of Buddy #2's jacket. He unfastens the Velcro closure over the zippered front of Buddy #2's jacket and unzips the jacket. Buddy #1 grasps Buddy #2's jacket by the shoulders and instructs him to make a fist. He then pulls the jacket down and away from Buddy #2, ensuring that the black part of the jacket is not touched. He lays Buddy #2's overgarment jacket on the ground, black side up. (It will be used to stand on later.) Buddy #1 carefully unfastens and unzips Buddy #2's trousers. Do not loosen Buddy #2's waist tabs.

He instructs Buddy #2 to break the seals on his overboots by alternately stepping on each heel and pulling up on his foot. He grasps Buddy #2's trousers and pulls them down to his knees. Buddy #1 instructs Buddy #2 to walk out of his trousers/overboots, taking care not to step on the contaminated side of the overgarment. If Buddy #2 is wearing overboots, Buddy #1 removes Buddy #2's trousers first and then helps him step out of his overboots onto the black side of the jacket. Buddy #2 should step onto the jacket wearing his mask, BDU, combat boots, and gloves.

Step 5—Remove Gloves

The soldier holds the fingertips of his gloves and partially slides his hand out. When the fingers of both hands are free, he holds his arms away from his body and lets the gloves drop.

Step 6—Put on Overgarment

Buddy #1 opens the package containing the new overgarment without touching the inside of the package. Buddy #2 pulls out the overgarment without touching the outside of the package. He puts on the overgarment and fastens it, leaving the trouser legs open. Do not reverse roles. Only Buddy #2 will put on the clean overgarments at this time.

Step 7—Put on Overboots and Gloves

Buddy #1 opens the package of clean overboots without touching the inside of the package. Buddy #2 removes the overboots without touching the outside of the package, puts them on, and fastens his trouser legs. Buddy #1 opens the package of clean gloves without touching the inside of the package. Buddy #2 removes the gloves without touching the outside of the package and puts them on. Buddy #2 puts on the M9 detector paper. Do not reverse roles. Only Buddy #2 will put on clean overboots and gloves at this time. The gloves and overboots will have a light powdery coating. This is normal. It is not necessary to remove it. It will not affect the protective qualities.

Step 8—Secure Hood

Buddy #1 wipes his rubber gloves with an IEDK. He unrolls Buddy #2's hood and attaches the straps and tightens the neck cord. He checks the clips and neck cord on Buddy #2's hood. Buddy #1 and Buddy #2 reverse roles and repeat steps 2 through 8.

Step 9—Secure Gear

The soldier secures his individual gear and puts it back on. He puts on a new chemical protective helmet cover and moves to the Assembly Area. He uses the buddy system to check the fit of all secured gear.

Individual (Emergency) Method

This method is used only when a soldier does not have a buddy to help him and the risk of MOPP gear failure demands that an exchange occur.

Step 1—Decon Gear

Removes gross contamination from individual gear (weapon, helmet, load carrying equipment, and mask carrier).

The soldier uses M8 detector paper to determine the areas of gross contamination and field-expedient absorbents (sand, dirt, or rags) to remove gross liquid contamination. He should take special care to avoid touching these areas during overgarment removal. He uses an IEDK to decon his individual gear (helmet, load carrying equipment, weapon, and mask carrier).

Step 2—Prepare to Decon

Facilitates removal of overgarment trousers and overboots.

The soldier unfastens the shoulder straps on his hood, pulls them over his shoulders, and reattaches them. He loosens the drawcord on the hood of his protective mask. If wearing the M43 protective mask, tie off the microphone cord to the hose of the mask. He removes the M9 detector paper from his overgarment and unties/cuts the drawcords on the trouser legs of his overgarment. He unzips the trouser legs and rolls a cuff in each trouser leg, ensuring that the cuffs do not come above the top of his overboots. He unfastens or cuts the fasteners on the overboots.

Step 3—Decon Mask and Hood

Removes gross contamination from the mask and hood.

The soldier wipes the eye-lens outserts on his mask from the top down. He wipes his mask and gloves and rolls his hood. He grasps the straps of the hood and lifts the hood off his shoulders and partially over his head until most of the back of his head is exposed. He rolls the hood, starting at the chin, and works around the entire mask until the rolled hood will stay up and off of his shoulders. He tucks the straps and neck cord into the roll. He rolls the hood tightly against his mask without pulling the hood off the back of his head. He tucks the tail between the upper part of the canister and the mask. Tie the tail over and under the hose for the M42 mask.

The soldier removes the applicator mitt from the package with his nondominant hand. Making a "V," he wipes down his hand, paying particular attention to the areas between his fingers. Once he has thoroughly wiped down his dominant hand, he must insert it into the applicator mitt and thoroughly wipe down his other hand. He gently pats the voicemitter with black powder until it is covered.

The soldier starts at the top of his hood and wipes down and away, patting until the surface of the hood is covered by the black powder. He rewipes his gloves, starting with his nondominant hand.

The soldier lifts the hood off his shoulders by grasping the shoulder straps in one hand and placing the other hand on top of the head and pulling the hood over his head until the elastic band is over his knuckles and most of the back of his head is exposed. He should not expose his ears or pull the hood completely over his face or mask. He tucks his shoulder straps, underarm straps, and the rolled portion of his hood under the elastic band.

Follow these procedures when using the M40A1 mask with the quick-doff hood. The soldier removes the underarm straps from the front of his hood and places them over his shoulders. He refastens them on the front of his hood. Anytime you decon your mask or roll your hood, place two fingers on the voicemitter of the mask to prevent accidental breakage of the seal.

Step 4—Remove Overgarments and Overboots

Prevents agent from penetrating to the undergarments or the skin.

The soldier grasps his overgarment jacket and unsnaps the snaps individually. He unties the drawcord at the bottom of the jacket. He unfastens the Velcro at the waist and then refastens it. He unfastens the Velcro closure over the zippered front of the jacket and unzips the jacket. He grasps the front of the jacket and pulls the jacket back until it is off his shoulders. He puts his arms behind his back and works his arms out of the sleeves. He should not let the outside of the jacket touch his body. When the jacket is off, he lays it on the ground with the black side up. He unfastens and unzips his trousers. He should not loosen his waist tabs. He loosens his overboots by alternately stepping on each heel and pulling up on his foot. He grasps his trousers and pushes them down to his knees. He walks out of his trousers/overboots simultaneously and steps onto the black side of the jacket. He steps onto the jacket wearing his mask, BDU, combat boots, and gloves.

Step 5—Remove Gloves

The soldier wipes around the edges of the packages containing the new items (gloves, overgarments, and overboots) with an IEDK. He opens the new packages. He holds the fingertips of his gloves and partially slides his hands out. When the fingers of both hands are free, he holds his arms away from his body and lets his gloves drop.

Step 6—Put on Overgarment

The soldier removes the overgarment from its package without touching the outside. He puts on the overgarment and fastens it, leaving the trouser legs open until he puts on the new overboots.

Step 7—Put on Overboots and Gloves

The soldier removes the overboots (one at a time) from their package without touching the outside and puts them on. He removes the gloves from their package without touching the outside, puts them on, and fastens his trouser legs. The gloves and overboots will have a light powdery coating. This is normal. Do not remove it. It will not affect the protective qualities.

Step 8—Secure Hood

The soldier secures his individual gear and puts it back on. He puts on a new chemical protective helmet cover and moves to the Assembly Area.

Step 9—Secure Gear

The soldier secures his individual gear and puts it back on. He puts on a new chemical protective helmet cover and moves to the Assembly Area.

Vehicle Wash-Down

A vehicle wash-down may be conducted with or without Power-Driven Decon Equipment (PDDE) and in either a one- or two-lane configuration. An unsupported wash-down requires the contaminated unit to have washing equipment that can produce 60 to 120 pounds per square inch (psi) of water pressure. The capacity to heat water and inject soap increases effectiveness of decontamination. A supported wash-down requires PDDE organic to the unit or from a supporting chemical decon or dual purpose company. A two-lane wash-down is simply a one-lane wash-down parallel with another (see Figure 4.1).

Other configurations for vehicle wash-down decontamination are limited only by the constraints of the time, location, and personnel. Figure 4.1 illustrates a typical operational decontamination setup. The vehicle wash-down process is as follows:

Step 1—Assemble Vehicles

Personnel at the control point supervise preparing vehicles and directing movement out of the marshaling area.

Step 2—Prepare Vehicles

Individual/crew closes all access doors, hatches, windows, and other openings. Remove camouflage and cover muzzles. If required, crews (less drivers) move to the MOPP gear exchange area. Move to the wash area is on order.

Figure 4.1
Operational-Decon Setup

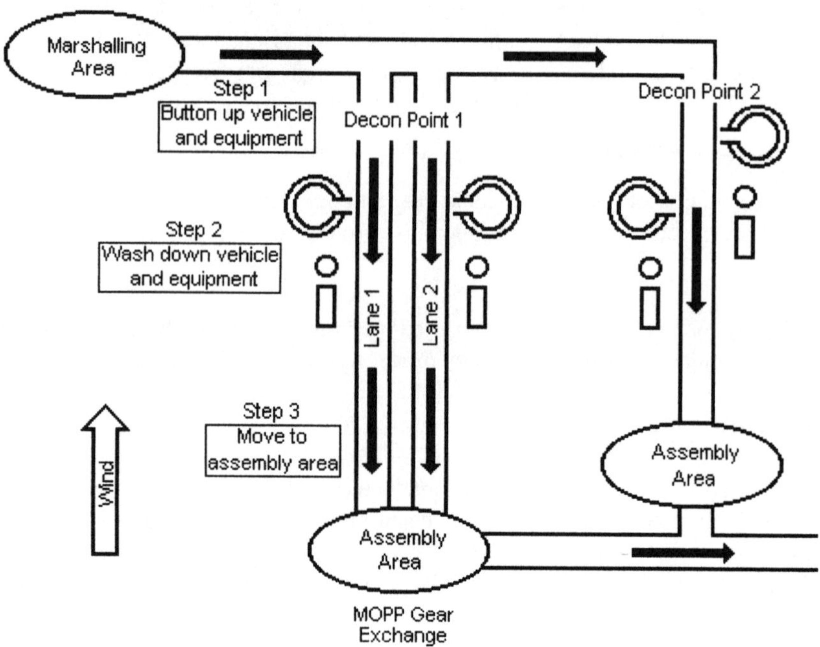

Step 3—Perform Wash-down

Soldiers/personnel wash equipment from top to bottom. Decontamination crew wears a Toxicological Apron, protective (TAP) or wet weather gear over MOPP gear.

Step 4—Move Out to the Next Position

Vehicles move to the MOPP gear exchange area (if required) or the next battle position.

Thorough Decontamination

Detailed Equipment Decontamination (DED) restore items so that they can be used without MOPP gear. Normally, the DED is conducted as part of a reconstitution or during breaks in combat operations. These operations require support from a chemical decontamination unit.

Detailed Troop Decontamination (DTD) normally takes place in conjunction with DED. The contaminated unit conducts this process and supports the DED operations. Figure 4.2 shows a typical configuration for a DED and DTD layout.

Figure 4.2
Typical Configuration for a DED and DTD Layout

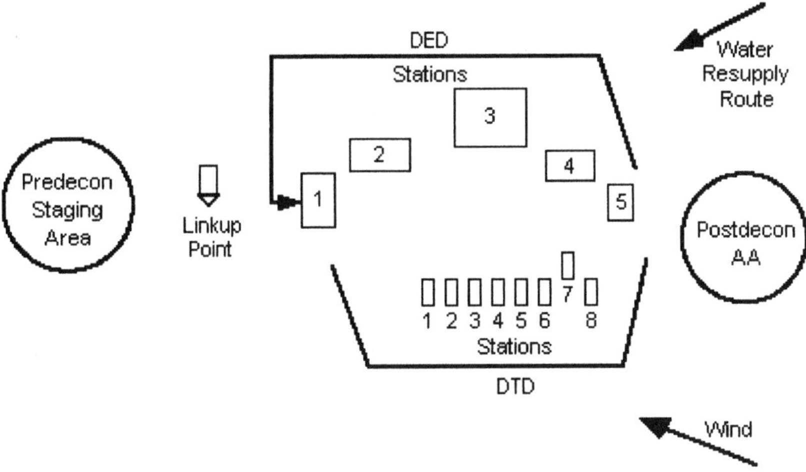

Detailed Equipment Decon

Chemical units are responsible for setting up, operating, and closing the DED portion of the thorough decon operation. The DED for chemical and biological contamination comprises of five stations. Stations are normally 98 to 164 feet (30 to 50 meters) apart; however, spacing is terrain-dependent.

Station 1—Primary Wash

1-1. At this station, the gross contamination and dirt are removed from the vehicle. The vehicle is sprayed for two to three minutes with hot, soapy water. The vehicle is then scrubbed to help remove caked-on dirt. The mechanical action of scrubbing also helps remove thickened chemical agents. Although the undersurfaces are difficult to reach, try to remove as much dirt as possible. After scrubbing the vehicle, spray it again for two to three minutes to remove loosened dirt and contamination. This station uses about 250 gallons of water per vehicle. Larger vehicles with large quantities of dirt use more water. The runoff from this station is contaminated and must be treated as hazardous. The contaminated runoff must be controlled; if available, engineer support may be used. This station requires high water-pressure systems (M12A1 Power Driven Decon Apparatus [PDDA] and M17 Lightweight Decontaminating System [LDS]) rather than low-water volume systems (65 - GPM pumps).

Note: Thirty-five cubic feet of space per 250 gallons of liquid runoff should be used when calculating the size for the drainage pump.

1-2. The effectiveness of the wash depends on the type of wash (hot, soapy water; hot water; cold water; or steam). Hot, soapy water is water-heated to about 120° to 140°F to which a detergent has been added to reduce its surface tension. The detergent removes the agent by emulsification, which is followed by the mechanical displacement of the suspension. Hot water alone is less effective than hot, soapy water. Because of the high temperature, some agents are best removed by steam through vaporization. Finally, for some chemical agents, cold water exhibits better solvent characteristics.

Station 2—Decontamination Solution 2 (DS2) Application

2-1. At this station, a decontaminant is applied to the entire vehicle. The vehicle is divided into four parts, and a member of the scrubbing team is assigned that part of the vehicle. This limits the workload of each member of the scrubbing team and avoids duplication of work. DS2 is applied starting at the top of the vehicle and working toward the undercarriage. Every effort is made to apply DS2 to the undercarriage, especially if the vehicle has crossed a contaminated area. The mop is the least tiring method of applying DS2. Using a mop to apply DS2 creates a large amount of spillage. However, with continual use of the M13 Decontaminating Apparatus, Portable (DAP) requires the scrubbing team to exert more energy than with using the mop. The M13 DAP can be used to apply DS2 to hard-to-reach areas.

2-2. Before starting the decon operation, the scrubbing team pours 5-gallon cans of DS2 into 30-gallon containers if mops are going to be used instead of M13 DAPs. Each member of the scrubbing team wears a TAP apron or wet-weather gear to protect himself from the DS2.

2-3. Water adversely affects the DS2's ability to react with chemical agents. If there is excess water remaining on the vehicle from station 1, the scrubbing team can

- Wait for the majority of the water to evaporate.
- Remove the excess water.
- Increase the amount of DS2 applied.

2-4. There must be sufficient DS2 on the item being decontaminated for complete neutralization to occur. The DS2-to-agent ratio needs to be 55 to 1 for H agents and 25 to 1 for G agents. For a vehicle the size of an M1A1 tank, this corresponds to 15 and 7 gallons, respectively.

Station 3—Contact Time/Interior Decon

3-1. At this station, the DS2 is allowed to completely neutralize the chemical agent, and the interior of the vehicle is decontaminated. Vehicles are moved to a concealed position. Vehicles will remain in station 3 for no less than 30 minutes. DS2 reacts with most chemical agents within 5 minutes. However, by allowing the DS2 to remain on the contaminated surface for 30 minutes, the amount of agent that will later desorb (off gas) will be significantly reduced. When there is a 30-minute contact time, there will be no desorption after decon operations for most chemical agents. However, studies indicate that distilled mustard (HD) vapors desorb after decon even if DS2 is allowed to remain for 30 minutes.

3-2. While the vehicle is held at this station for the DS2 to completely react, the driver inspects the interior of the vehicle for liquid contamination. He is given M8 detector paper to check for chemical contamination. If he identifies chemical contamination, he is given decon supplies to decon the interior of the vehicle. The best decon solution for use in the interior of vehicles is a 5% solution of HTH or STB. The driver wipes all reasonably accessible surfaces with a rag or sponge soaked in the HTH or STB solution. He should not attempt to decon areas where there is little likelihood of contamination (electrical assemblies, area beneath the turret floor, and so forth).

3-3. Once the interior decon is completed, the driver places a cover over the seat and floor of the vehicle. Then he dismounts from the vehicle and proceeds to the start of the DTD. The assistant driver, having completed the DTD, mounts the vehicle and moves it to the next station. Drivers must exercise caution when entering or exiting the vehicle. A DS2-coated surface is slippery, and the DS2 may react with chemical protective footwear. Personnel should avoid stepping in DS2 and tracking it into the vehicle.

CAUTION
Do not mix HTH or STB with DS2.
If mixed, a violent reaction will occur.

Station 4—Rinse

4-1. At this station, the DS2 is removed from the vehicle. The vehicle is sprayed with water from top to bottom. Take care to rinse the undercarriage. This station uses about 200 gallons of water per vehicle. Failure to remove all DS2 from the vehicle may cause a false positive reading at station 5. If high water-pressure systems (M12A1 PDDA and M17 LDS) are not available, large-volume water pumps (65 GPM pumps) should be used at this station. The driver removes plastic or other material (if present) covering the seats and floor and disposes of it as hazardous waste.

Station 5—Check

5-1. At this station, the vehicle is checked to see if it has a negligible contamination level or if it still has significant contamination remaining. Detection procedures will vary depending on the type of contamination. If significant contamination is found on the vehicle, the vehicle will be recycled to station 2 for chemical contamination. An assistant driver takes the vehicle to the Assembly Area.

5-2. The CAM is used to check for the presence of vapor from residual liquid contamination. A one-bar or lower reading on the CAM indicates a negligible contamination level. Once the CAM indicates the presence of vapor contamination, M8 detector paper is used to verify the presence of liquid contamination. If it is suspected that both the CAM and M8 detector paper are producing a false positive, use an M256A1 detector kit to confirm or deny the presence of contamination. If the vehicle has significant contamination remaining, recycle it. The commander may modify the recycle criteria based on mission requirements.

The commander, with the chemical unit leader's help, establishes the recycle criteria before starting decon operations. The recycle criteria determine which vehicles will return to station 2 after contamination is detected at station 5. If the unit has sufficient time and resources, any vehicle having more contamination than the acceptable level should be recycled. However, time and resources are usually limited, and not all vehicles can be recycled. The recycle criteria are based on the weathering effects.

5-3. There will be desorption of chemical agents from the surfaces after decon. The desorption of vapors on surfaces painted with the Chemical Agent Resistant Coating (CARC) will stop sooner then those surfaces painted with alkyd paints. Consider this when checking decontaminated items for overall decon effectiveness.

Detailed Troop Decon (DTD)

The contaminated unit or its higher headquarters (HQ) is responsible for setting up, operating, manning, and closing the DTD area at the thorough decon site. The chemical unit leader determines the general location of the DTD within the decon site and provides technical advice on setting up, operating, and closing the DTD area. The supervisor of the DTD must establish a work/rest cycle. There are eight stations for a DTD. Spacing between the stations is 10 to 16 feet. Table 4.3 summarizes the equipment and supplies needed for each DTD station.

Table 4.3
Equipment/Supplies Needed for DTD

Stations	Equipment/Supplies
Station 1 - Individual Gear Decon	1 monitor (CAM operator) 4 30-gallon containers 2 long-handled brushes 2 ponchos or plastic sheets 1 CAM 8 books of M8 detector paper 4 M256A1 detector kits 100 plastic trash bags Sufficient STB slurry mix Rinse water
Station 2 - Overboots and Hood Decon	Cutting tool One SKD or IEDK per person Large plastic sheet Plastic trash bags (as required) 10 drums of STB1 shovel
Station 3 - Overgarment Removal	2 30-gallon containers 100 plastic trash bags 10 boxes of SDKs
Station 4 - Overboot and Glove Removal	8 30-gallon containers 2 long-handled brushes M8 detector paper (as required) 1 immersion heater 100 plastic trash bags 1 CAM Engineer tape 1 cutting tool 2 Ponchos or large plastic sheets 10% STB/HTH solution Hot, soapy water Cold rinse water
Station 5 - Monitor	1 CAM First aid supplies 5 books of M8 detector papers 1 case of SDKs
Station 6 - Mask Removal	1 M8A1 or M22 ACAA Engineer tape
Station 7 - Mask Decon Point	1 30-gallon container 4 3-gallon containers 1 CAM 2 sponges One case of paper towels 1 immersion heater Mask sanitizing solution

	Hot, soapy water Rinse water
Station 8 - Reissue Point	Mask PLL

Station 1—Individual Gear Decon

1-1. At this station, contamination is removed from individual gear (LCE, mask carrier, helmet, and weapon) to a negligible risk level.

1-2. Dig a sump that is six feet long, six feet wide, and four feet deep (minimum). Place three 30-gallon containers near the sump for ease of changing. Fill two containers with an STB slurry mix. Fill the other two containers with clean water for rinsing and place it about three feet forward of the STB cans. Place two long-handled scrub brushes at each can of STB slurry.

1-3. To prepare the slurry, mix 100 pounds of STB with 20 gallons of hot water. The chemical unit provides the hot water. Change the mixture after 20 soldiers have decontaminated their gear. The rinse water should be changed after every 10 soldiers or when it appears dirty (place the waste mixture in the sump).

1-4. Place a poncho or a plastic sheet on the ground at the checkpoint. Divide the poncho or the sheet in half using engineer tape. This is the contamination control line. The checkpoint will be a minimum of 10 feet from all other stations in order to get a true reading on the detection equipment.

1-5. Three soldiers are required to operate this station. One soldier supervises the decon of the individual gear and takes the decontaminated equipment to the checkpoint. He also prepares a new slurry mixture as necessary. One soldier remains at the checkpoint and checks all the gear using the detection equipment to ensure that it is decontaminated. One soldier transports the decontaminated gear to the reissue point.

1-6. The soldier decontaminates his gear by washing and scrubbing it for six minutes in a decontaminant container with hot, soapy water or an STB slurry mix. If he is wearing the M42 mask, he should use hot, soapy water and a sponge or an STB slurry mix to decon the hose and canister.

1-7. The soldier dips his gear into the clean water and rinses it for four minutes and then hands it to the attendant and proceeds to the next station. The attendant takes the gear to the equipment checkpoint and places the decontaminated gear on the "dirty" side of the contamination control line and returns to the containers to pick up more gear. The monitor at the checkpoint checks the gear using the appropriate detection device and the procedures associated with that device. If the residual contamination exceeds negligible risks, recycle the gear and decon it again. If the gear passes the check, place it on the clean side of the contamination control line. The attendant will carry the equipment to the reissue point.

1-8. Depending on the time available, more extensive washing and checking procedures may be used. The longer the gear is washed or left out in the air after washing, the lower the contamination level. The gear may be put in closed areas or plastic bags and checked for hazardous vapors with the M256A1 detector kit or the CAM. The CAM detects only the G series nerve agent vapors and the H series blister agent vapors.

1-9. If this step is not done properly, contamination may remain on the equipment. The resulting vapor hazard could cause casualties to unmasked personnel, particularly in closed areas (vehicle interiors) or heavily wooded areas where air circulation is poor.

Station 2—Overboot and Hood Decon

2-1. At this station, gross contamination on overboots, trouser legs, mask, and hood is neutralized. If ample hoods are available at the reissue point, the hood should be cut away.

2-2. Prepare a shuffle pit by digging a shallow pit about three feet long, three feet wide, and six inches deep. Fill the shuffle pit with an STB dry mix or an STB slurry, depending on water availability. Prepare the STB dry mix by mixing three parts of earth to two parts of STB. Prepare the STB slurry in the same manner as at station 1 (see step 1-3). Add more STB to the mix after 10 soldiers have processed through the shuffle pit. The chemical unit will provide 10 drums of STB for every company-sized unit that goes through the station.

2-3. One soldier is required to operate this station. The attendant directs and "observes" the soldiers as they decon their overboots and hoods.

2-4. The soldier walks into the shuffle pit and spreads his legs apart (double shoulder width), bends at the waist, and uses his hands to thoroughly rub the STB dry mix or the STB slurry on his overboots and lower trouser legs. He should take special care to rub the rear of his overboots. He should also remove any excess decontaminant from his gloves.

2-5. If a replacement hood is available, remove the hood as follows. Buddy #1 cuts the shoulder straps and drawcord on Buddy #2's hood. Buddy #1 pulls Buddy #2's hood inside-out over the front of the mask, being careful not to touch the exposed neck or head. Buddy #1 gathers Buddy #2's hood in one hand, and using a cutting tool, cuts away the hood as close as possible to the eye-lens outsert, voicemitter, and inlet valve covers. Make sure nothing is left dangling below the bottom of the mask.

2-6. If a replacement hood is not available, Buddy #1 decontaminates and rolls Buddy #2's hood in the same manner as for a MOPP gear exchange. When the task is completed, Buddy #1 and Buddy #2 reverse roles. Soldiers should check their overboots, rubber gloves, and overgarment for damage. Any rips, tears, or punctures in these items should be reported to the monitor at station 5.

This allows the monitor at station 5 to check the soldiers for chemical agent symptoms and their clothing for possible contamination.

2-7. If this step is not done properly, contamination can be transferred to the combat boots and the head and neck area from the hood.

Station 3—Overgarment Removal

3-1. At this station, contaminated overgarments are removed before the agent penetrates the overgarment material and touches the undergarments or the skin.

3-2. One soldier is required to operate this station. He directs and "monitors" the soldiers as they remove their overgarments in the same manner as a MOPP gear exchange.

3-3. The attendant assists the soldier in removing his overgarment. The attendant cuts and removes the M9 detector paper from around the soldier's wrist. He unfastens the Velcro closure over the jacket zipper, waist cord, and wrist Velcro straps on the soldier's jacket. He unfastens the back snaps and instructs the soldier to make a fist. He then pulls the soldier's jacket down and away from him.

3-4. The attendant cuts and removes the M9 detector paper from the soldier's trousers. He unfastens the Velcro straps and zippers on the cuffs of the soldier's trousers. He also unfastens the front waist snaps and unzips the front zipper. He has the soldier lift one leg and point that foot down and bend slightly at the knees for stability. The attendant grasps the cuff of the elevated foot with a hand on each side and pulls the cuff in an alternating, jerking motion until the soldier can step out of the trouser leg. The process is repeated on the other leg. The attendant ensures that the soldier steps wide enough so as not to rub his clean leg against the contaminated boot and overgarment.

3-5. If this step is not done properly, the agent may be transferred to the undergarment or the skin.

Station 4—Overboot and Glove Removal

4-1. At this station, contaminated overboots and gloves are removed to limit the spread of contamination. The overboots and gloves may also be decontaminated for reissue (if serviceable).

4-2. If the overboots and gloves are not being decontaminated, two 30-gallon containers are needed. If replacement overboots and gloves are available, establish a liquid contamination control line and set two 30-gallon containers one foot back from the line. Soldiers support themselves using the containers and discard their overgarments into the containers. An attendant directs and monitors the soldiers as they remove their overboots and gloves in the same manner as a MOPP gear exchange; however, the soldiers step over the control line instead of onto a jacket.

4-3. If replacement overboots and gloves are not available, set up the station as follows: Fill two 30-gallon containers with hot, soapy water and two 30-gallon containers with a 10% STB/HTH solution, placing two scrub brushes near the containers. Then fill two 30-gallon containers with cold rinse water. One attendant supervises and assists the soldiers wearing the M42 mask. The other two attendants decon the overboots and the gloves; one processes the overboots, while the other processes the gloves. Note: Replace the water in the container once 20 items have been processed. When available, the decon platoon will assist with the water requirements.

4-4. For both situations, use engineer tape to mark the liquid-contamination control line on the ground. Place the cutting tools, two containers, and plastic bags on the "dirty" side of the liquid-contamination control line. The liquid-contamination control line separates the "dirty" and "clean" areas. No liquid agent should be tracked on the ground beyond the liquid-contamination control line.

4-5. The liquid-contamination control line separates the “dirty” and “clean” areas. The attendant unfastens or cuts the elastic closures on the soldier’s overboots. The soldier faces the liquid-contamination control line and steps back from it about 12 inches. The attendant steps on the back of the soldier’s overboot and instructs him to lift his heel and work his foot out of the overboot and step across the liquid-contamination control line. Repeat the process on the other foot. If the overboot cannot be removed by this process, the attendant cuts it off and discards it in the designated container. The soldier holds the fingertips of his gloves and partially slides his hands out. The attendant remove the soldier’s gloves.

4-6. If the soldier is wearing the M42 protective mask, the attendant from station 6 carries the soldier’s filter canister until it is removed. The attendant at station 4 performs his duty from the “dirty” side of the liquid-contamination control line.

4-7. The overboots and gloves are decontaminated using the following steps. Check all items for holes, tears, and punctures and discard any item with this defect. Do not decon any item that is unserviceable.

- Step 1. Submerge the gloves and overboots in their respective container of hot, soapy water. Some of the contamination is removed during this step. When the overboots and gloves are removed from the container, ensure that no water remains inside them.
- Step 2. Submerge the gloves and overboots in their respective containers of STB/HTH solution. Thoroughly scrub the items until no visible contamination remains. After scrubbing, submerge each item once more before moving to the rinse container.

- Step 3. Thoroughly rinse the scrubbed items, making sure that they are rinsed inside as well as outside.
- Step 4. Place usable items on a poncho or a plastic sheet to air-dry and weather.
- Step 5. Place usable items in plastic trash bags along with an M256A1 detector kit. If the detector kit shows contamination remaining, the attendants can recycle the items or discard them. However, if the kit show no contamination, the items can be reused.

4-8. If the overboots are not properly removed, the combat boots may become contaminated, and contamination may be spread to clean areas. If the gloves are not properly removed, the undergarments and skin may become contaminated.

Station 5—Monitor

5-1. At this station, contamination on personnel is identified, spot decon capabilities are provided, and medical aid is provided, as required.

5-2. Medical personnel should be present to treat any soldiers suffering from chemical agent symptoms.

5-3. The attendant checks the soldiers for contamination using the CAM. Liquid agents can be detected with M8 detector paper. Small quantities of agent vapor can be detected with the CAM. Symptoms of agent poisoning are the most obvious indication of skin contamination. At this station, the medic checks each soldier for symptoms of agent poisoning and treats, as required. Soldiers should report any damage to their MOPP gear that was identified at stations 2, 3, and 4. The attendant can decon any areas identified as contaminated with an SDK. Soldiers are remonitored after decon. It is possible that all liquid chemical contamination is absorbed into the clothing. If so, M8/M9 detector paper will indicate negative, even though there is a hazard.

5-4. If this station is omitted, the soldier could become a casualty. After this station, the soldier is not checked for contamination or decontamined again. Commanders can choose to conduct more extensive contamination checks here if medical assistance and time are available. This decreases the risk of casualties.

Station 6—Mask Removal

6-1. At this station, the mask is removed without contaminating the soldier. The mask is taken to a mask decon point, limiting agent transfer at the station.

6-2. If the hood is still attached to the mask, the attendant pulls the hood over the front of the mask, grabs the mask by the voicemitter cover, and pulls the mask off the soldier. The soldier holds his breath as the mask is removed. If the mask has optical inserts, the attendant holds the mask open so that the soldier can remove the inserts without touching the outside of the mask. The soldier walks upwind 16 feet, crosses the vapor contamination control line, and then resumes breathing. The attendant brings the mask to station 7.

6-3. If the wind direction remains constant, no chemical vapor hazard is expected beyond the vapor-contamination control line. Position the M8A1 or the M22 Automatic Chemical Agent Alarm (ACAA) upwind of the station to warn of vapor hazards. The soldier getting decontaminated moves straight ahead while his mask, which may still give off vapors, is held on the vapor dirty side of the line and taken to station 7, where it is decontaminated.

6-4. If the step is not done properly, the soldier could breathe toxic vapors. There is a high probability that the vapor hazard is still present on the mask and the hood. The soldier must not touch the outside of the mask because it could contaminate his bare hands.

Station 7—Mask Decon Point

7-1. At this station, all the contamination is removed from the mask. Once 20 items have been processed in the wash containers, replace the water. Once 10 items have been processed in the rinse water, replace it. Place the contaminated waste into the sump.

7-2. Dig a sump that is four feet long, four feet wide, and four feet deep in which to discard used filters and canisters. Three soldiers are needed to operate this station. Two soldiers strip, wash, rinse, sanitize, and dry masks. The other soldier checks the masks and carries them to the reissue point.

7-3. Remove the eye-lens outserts and the hood if the hood was not cut off at station 2. Remove and discard the filters or canisters. Put the items into the properly marked containers. Wash the mask, hood, eye-lens outserts, and the hoses on the M42 and M43 masks in hot, soapy water. Rinse these items in clean water, dip them into the sanitizing solution, agitate them for five minutes, and then rinse them again in clean water. Add one tube of mask sanitizing solution (calcium hypochlorite) to each quart of water. Wipe the masks with rags until they are almost dry. Discard each container of mask sanitizing solution into a sump after every 10 masks. The attendant checks the masks for contamination with a CAM. If the masks are still contaminated, the attendant recycles them for more decon and then decons his rubber gloves. If the masks are not contaminated, the attendant takes the masks to the reissue point. The attendant must take care not to contaminate the reissue point or himself.

7-4. If this step is not done properly, the soldiers may become contaminated when the masks are reissued to them at the reissue point. Even though the step is done correctly, there is still a possible danger when many masks are stacked together. Small amounts of residual vapor from each mask can become potentially dangerous. Runners between stations 7 and 8 are in MOPP 2 and are prepared to go into MOPP 4.

Station 8—Reissue Point

8-1. At this station, the mask with its components is provided to the soldier for reassembly.

8-2. At this station, the Protective-Mask Prescribed Load-List parts are needed. The unit Nuclear, Biological, and Chemical (NBC) Non-Comissioned Officer (NCO)/supply sergeant sets up the reissue point to provide the soldiers with replacement parts for all types of protective masks and assist in mask maintenance.

8-3. The mask with its components is reissued to the soldier, who assembles it in the assembly area. The unit chemical NCO affixes canisters to the cleaned M42 and M43 hoses. The soldier picks up individual gear and moves to the postdecon assembly area.

8-4. If this step is not done properly, the soldier may be inadequately equipped for future operations. If time is not available, the NBC NCO will have replacement chemical suits, overboots, and gloves at this station for reissue. If time is available, personnel will receive this equipment at the postdecon assembly area.

Litter Patient Decontamination

Before patients receive medical treatment in the clean treatment area, an eight-man patient decon team decontaminates them.

Figure 4.3 shows one way to establish the patient-decon station. Place the bandage scissors in a container of 5% chlorine solution between each use.

The team members decon their gloves and aprons with a 5 percent chlorine solution. Note that litter patients requiring Emergency Medical Treatment (EMT) or Ambulatory Medical Treatment (AMT) in the clean area of the Medical Treatment Facility (MTF) will be completely decontaminated. However, a patient requiring immediate evacuation should have only his wound area and MOPP gear spot-decontaminated to remove any gross contamination (e.g., a stable patient with a partial amputation of a lower extremity). The patient should be evacuated in his MOPP gear.

Decon the patient's skin, bandages, wounds, mask, identification tags with chain, and splints by wiping them with a 0.5% chlorine solution.

Some procedures in the following steps can be done with one soldier, while others require more than one soldier.

Figure 4.3
Layout for a Patient-Decon Station and Clean Treatment Area

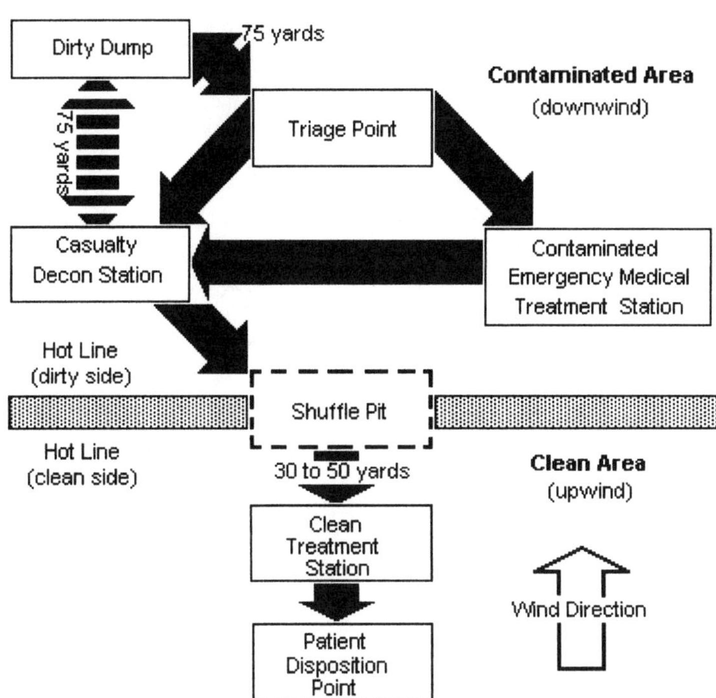

Step 1—Decon the Patient's Mask and Hood

1-1. Move the patient to the clothing removal station. After the patient has been triaged and stabilized (if necessary) by the senior medic in the patient-decon area, move him to the litter stands at the clothing removal station.

1-2. Decon the hood. Use either an IEDK or a 5% chlorine solution (or household bleach) to wipe down the front, sides, and top of the hood.

1-3. Remove the hood. Remove the hood by cutting it with scissors or by loosening it from the mask attachment points for the quick-doff hood or other similar hoods. Before cutting the hood, dip the scissors in a 5% chlorine solution. Cut the neck cord and the small string under the voicemitter. Release or cut the hood shoulder straps and unzip the hood zipper. Cut the hood upward to the top of the eye-lens outsert, staying close to the filter-inlet cover and eye-lens outsert, then across the forehead to the outer edge of the other eye-lens outsert. Proceed downward toward the patient's shoulder, staying close to the eye-lens outsert and filter-inlet cover, then across the lower part of the voicemitter to the zipper. After dipping the scissors in the 5% chlorine solution, cut the hood from the center of the forehead over the top of the head. Fold the left and right sides of the hood to the side of the patient's head, laying the sides of the hood on the litter.

1-4. Decon the protective mask and exposed skin. Use an SDK or a 0.5% chlorine solution to wipe the external parts of the mask. Cover the mask's air inlets with gauze or your hand to keep the mask filter dry. Continue by wiping the exposed areas of the patient's face, to include the neck and behind the ears. Do not remove the protective mask.

1-5. Remove the Field Medical Card (FMC). Cut the patient's FMC tie wire, allowing the FMC to fall into a plastic bag. Seal the plastic bag and rinse the outside of the bag with a 5% chlorine solution. Place the plastic bag under the back of the protective mask's head straps. The FMC will remain with the patient in the contaminated area, and a clean copy will be made before the patient is moved to the clean area.

Step 2—Remove Gross Contamination from Protective Overgarment

2-1. Remove all visible contamination spots from the overgarment with an SDK or a 5% chlorine solution.

Step 3—Remove Personal Effects and Protective Overgarment

3-1. Remove the patient's personal effects. Remove the patient's personal effects from his protective overgarment and BDU pockets. Place the articles in a plastic bag, label the bag with the patient's identification, and seal the bag. If the articles are not contaminated, they are returned to the patient. If the articles are contaminated, place them in the contaminated holding area until they can be decontaminated, then return them to the patient. The overgarment jacket and trousers will be cut simultaneously. One soldier cuts the jacket, while another soldier cuts the trousers.

3-2. Cut and remove the overgarment jacket. Before cutting the overgarment jacket and trousers, dip the scissors in a 5% chlorine solution to prevent contamination of the patient's BDU or undergarments. Make two cuts, one up each sleeve from the wrist up to the shoulder and then across the shoulder through the collar. Cut around bandages, tourniquets, and splints, leaving them in place. Do not allow your gloves to touch the patient along the cut line. Keep the cuts close to the inside of the arms so that most of the sleeve material can be folded outward. Unzip the jacket and roll the chest sections to the respective sides, with the inner surface outward. Continue by tucking the clothing between the arm and chest. Roll the cut sleeves away from the arms, exposing the black liner.

3-3. Cut and remove the overgarment trousers. Cut both trousers legs starting at the ankle. Keep the cuts near the inside of the legs, along the inseam, to the crotch. With the left leg, cut all the way to the waist, avoiding the pockets. With the right leg, cut across at the crotch to the left leg cut. Cut around bandages, tourniquets, and splints, leaving them in place. Place the scissors in a 5% chlorine solution. Fold the cut trouser halves away from the patient and allow the halves to drop to the litter with the contaminated (green) side down. Roll the inner leg portion under and between the legs.

3-4. Remove the outer gloves. Before touching the patient, the patient-decon team decontaminates its gloves with a 5% chlorine solution. Lift the patient's arms up and out of the cutaway sleeves unless detrimental to his condition. Grasp the fingers of the gloves, roll the cuffs over the fingers, and turn the gloves inside out. Do not remove the inner cotton gloves at this time. Carefully lower the patient's arms across the chest after the outer gloves have been removed. Do not allow the patient's arms to come into contact with the exterior of his overgarment. Drop his gloves into the contaminated-waste bag. The team members decon their gloves with the 5% chlorine solution.

3-5. Remove the overboots. Cut the overboot laces and fold the lacing eyelets flat outward. While standing at the foot of the litter, hold the patient's heel with one hand. Pull the overboot downward, then toward you to remove it. Remove the two overboots simultaneously. This reduces the likelihood of contaminating one of the combat boots.

3-6. While holding the patient's heels off the litter, have a team member wipe the end of the litter with a 5% chlorine solution to neutralize any contamination that was transferred to the litter from the overboots. Lower the patient's heels onto the decontaminated litter. Place the overboots in the contaminated-waste bag. The team members decon their gloves with the 5% chlorine solution.

Step 4—Remove the Patient's BDU and Undergarments

4-1. Cut and remove the BDU. To cut and remove the BDU jacket and trousers, follow the procedures for removing the protective overgarment as described in paragraphs 3-2 and 3-3.

4-2. Remove the combat boots. Cut the bootlaces along the tongue. Remove the boots by pulling them toward you. Place the boots in the contaminated-waste bag. Do not touch the patient's skin with your contaminated gloves when removing his boots.

4-3. Cut and remove the undergarments. Follow the procedures for cutting away the protective overgarment and rolling it away from the patient (see paragraphs 3-2 and 3-3). Remove the socks and cotton gloves. Do not remove the identification tags.

Step 5—Transfer the Patient to a Decon Litter

5-1. After the patient's clothing has been cut away, transfer him to a decon litter or a canvas litter with a plastic-sheeting cover. Three decon team members decon their gloves and aprons with a 5% chlorine solution. One member places his hands under the patient's legs at the thighs and Achilles tendons, a second member places his arms under the patient's back and buttocks, and a third member places his arms under the patient's shoulders and supports the head and neck. They carefully lift the patient using their knees (not their backs) to minimize back strain. While the patient is elevated, another decon team member removes the litter from the litter stands and replaces it with a decontaminated (clean) litter. The team members carefully lower the patient onto the clean litter. The clothing and overgarments are placed in a contaminated-waste bag and moved to the contaminated-waste dump. The dirty litter is rinsed with the 5% chlorine solution and placed in the litter storage area.

Step 6—Decon the Patient's Skin

6-1. Spot-decon. With the patient in a supine position, spot-decon the skin by using an SDK or a 0.5% chlorine solution. Decon areas of potential contamination, to include areas around the neck, wrists, and lower parts of the face. Decon the patient's identification tags and chain, if necessary.

A complete body wash is not appropriate and may be harmful to the patient. During a complete body wash, the patient would have to be rolled over to reach all areas of the skin. This is not necessary for an adequate decon.

6-2. Combat medic care. The combat medic gently cuts away the bandage. He decontaminates the area around the wound and irrigates it with a 0.5% chlorine solution. If bleeding begins, he replaces the bandage with a clean one. He replaces the old tourniquet by placing a new one ½ to 1 inch above the old one. He then removes the old tourniquet and decontaminates the patient's skin with an SDK or a 0.5% chlorine solution. He does not remove a splint. He decontaminates the splint by thoroughly rinsing it, to include the padding and cravats, with a 0.5% chlorine solution.

6-3. Completeness of decon check. Check the patient with M8 detector paper or the CAM for completeness of decon. (Other monitoring devices may be used, if available.)

6-4. Contaminated-waste disposal. Dispose of contaminated bandages and coverings by placing them in a contaminated-waste bag. Seal the bag and place it in the contaminated-waste dump.

Step 7—Transfer the Patient Across the Shuffle Pit

7-1. The patient's clothing has been cut away, and his skin, bandages, and splints have been decontaminated. Transfer the patient to the shuffle pit and place the litter on the litter stands. The shuffle pit is wide enough to prevent the decon team members from straddling it while carrying the litter. A third team member will assist with transferring the patient to a clean treatment litter in the shuffle pit. Decon personnel rinse or wipe down their aprons and gloves with a 5% chlorine solution.

7-2. The three team members lift the patient off the decon litter (see step 5 for lifting procedures). While the patient is elevated, another team member removes the litter from the stands and returns it to the decon area. A medic from the clean side of the shuffle pit replaces the litter with a clean one. The patient is lowered onto the clean litter. Two medics from the clean side of the shuffle pit move the patient to the clean treatment area. The patient is treated in this area or awaits processing into the CPS. The litter is wiped down with a 5% chlorine solution in preparation for reuse. Once the patient is in the air lock of the CPS and the air lock has been purged, his protective mask is removed. Place the mask in a plastic bag and seal it.

Ambulatory Patient Decontamination

All ambulatory patients requiring EMT or AMT in the clean treatment area will be decontaminated. Stable patients not requiring treatment but requiring evacuation to the medical company's clearing station or a corps hospital for treatment (e.g., a patient with a broken arm), should be evacuated in their protective overgarments and masks by any available transportation. However, before evacuation, spot remove all thickened agents from their protective clothing.

Place the bandage scissors that are used in this procedure in a container of 5% chlorine solution when not in use. Most ambulatory patients will be treated in the contaminated treatment area and returned to duty. Upon removal of an ambulatory patient's clothing, he becomes a litter patient. The clearing station does not have clothing to replace those that are cut off during the decon process. The patient must be placed in a Patient Protective Wrap (PPW) for protection during evacuation (Figure 4.4).

The ambulatory patient is decontaminated and undressed as follows. Some procedures in the following steps can be done with one soldier, while others require more than one.

Step 1—Remove the LCE (Load-Carrying Equipment)

1-1. Remove the LCE by unfastening/unbuttoning all connectors or tie straps and then place the equipment in a plastic bag. Place the plastic bag in the designated storage area for later decon.

Figure 4.4
Chemical Agent Patient Protective Wrap

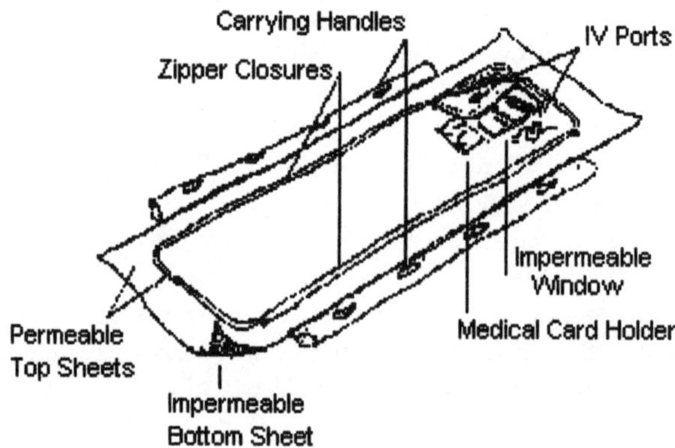

Step 2—Decon the Patient's Mask and Hood

2-1. Begin the clothing removal process. After the patient has been triaged and treated (if necessary) by the senior medic in the patient-decon station, the clothing removal process begins.

2-2. Decon the hood. Use either an IEDK or a 5% chlorine solution (or household bleach) to wipe down the front, sides, and top of the hood.

2-3. Remove the hood. Remove the hood by cutting it with scissors or by loosening it from the mask attachment points for the quick-doff hood or other similar hoods. Before cutting the hood, dip the scissors in a 5% chlorine solution. Cut the neck cord and the small string under the voicemitter. Release or cut the hood shoulder straps and unzip the hood zipper. Cut the hood upward to the top of the eye-lens outsert, staying close to the filter-inlet cover and eye-lens outsert, then across the forehead to the outer edge of the other eye-lens outsert. Proceed downward toward the patient's shoulder, staying close to the eye-lens outsert and filter-inlet cover, then across the lower part of the voicemitter to the zipper. After dipping the scissors in the 5% chlorine solution, cut the hood from the center of the forehead over the top of the head. Fold the left and right sides of the hood away from the patient's head and remove the hood.

2-4. Decon the protective mask and exposed skin. Decon the mask and the patient's face by using an SDK or a 0.5% chlorine solution. Cover the mask's air inlets with gauze or your hands to keep the mask filters dry. Continue by wiping the exposed areas of the patient's face, to include the neck and behind the ears. Do not remove the protective mask.

2-5. Remove the FMC. Cut the patient's FMC tie wire, allowing the FMC to fall into a plastic bag. Seal the plastic bag and rinse the outside of the bag with a 5% chlorine solution. Place the plastic bag under the back of the protective mask's head straps. The FMC will remain with the patient in the contaminated area, and a clean copy will be made before the patient is moved to the clean area.

Step 3—Remove Gross Contamination from Protective Overgarment

3-1. Remove all visible contamination spots from the overgarment by using an SDK (preferred method) or a 0.5% chlorine solution.

Step 4—Remove Personal Effects and Protective Overgarment

4-1. Remove the patient's personal effects. Remove the patient's personal effects from his protective overgarment and BDU pockets. Place the articles in a plastic bag, label the bag with the patient's identification, and seal the bag. If the articles are not contaminated, they are returned to the patient. If the articles are contaminated, place them in the contaminated holding area until they can be decontaminated; then return them to the patient.

4-2. Remove the overgarment jacket. Have the patient stand with his feet spread apart at shoulder width. Unsnap the front flap of the jacket and unzip the jacket. If the patient can extend his arms, have him clench his fists and extend his arms backward at about a 30° angle. Move behind the patient, grasp his jacket collar at the sides of the neck, and peel the jacket off the shoulders at a 30° angle down and away from the patient. Avoid any rapid or sharp jerks, which spread contamination. Gently pull the inside sleeves over the patient's wrists and hands.

4-3. If the patient cannot extend his arms, you must cut the jacket to aid in its removal. Before cutting the overgarment jacket, dip the scissors in a 5% chlorine solution to prevent contamination of the patient's BDU or underclothing. As with the litter patient, make two cuts, one up each sleeve from the wrist up to the shoulder and then across the shoulder through the collar. Cut around bandages, tourniquets, and splints, leaving them in place. Do not allow your gloves to touch the patient along the cut line. Peel the jacket back and downward to avoid spreading contamination. Ensure that the outside of the jacket does not touch the patient or his inner clothing.

4-4. Cut and remove the overgarment trousers. Unfasten or cut all ties, buttons, or zippers before grasping the trousers at the waist and peeling them down over the patient's combat boots. Again, the trousers are cut to aid in removal. If necessary, cut both trouser legs starting at the ankle. Keep the cuts near the inside of the legs, along the inseam, to the crotch. Cut around all bandages, tourniquets, and splints. Continue to cut up both sides of the zipper to the waist and allow the narrow strip with the zipper to drop between the legs. Peel or allow the trouser halves to drop to the ground. Have the patient step out of the trouser legs one at a time. Place the trousers in the contaminated-waste bag. Place the scissors in a 5% chlorine solution.

4-5. Remove the outer gloves. Grasp the fingers of the gloves, roll the cuffs over the fingers, and turn the gloves inside out. Do not remove the inner cotton gloves at this time. Drop the gloves into the contaminated-waste bag. Do not allow the patient to touch his clothing or other contaminated objects with his hands.

4-6. Remove the overboots. Cut the overboot laces and fold the lacing eyelets flat on the ground. Step on the toe and heel eyelets to hold the overboot on the ground and have the patient step out of it. Repeat this procedure for the other overboot. If the overboots are in good condition, they can be decontaminated and reissued.

4-7. Remove the patient's cotton glove liners. Instruct the patient to remove his cotton glove liners to reduce the possibility of spreading contamination. Have the patient grasp the heel of one glove liner with the other gloved hand, peeling it off his hand. Hold the removed glove by the inside and grasp the heel of the other glove, peeling it off his hand. Place both gloves in the contaminated waste-bag.

Step 5—Check the Patient for Contamination

5-1. After the patient's overgarment has been removed, check his BDU by using M8 detector paper or the CAM. Carefully survey the patient, paying particular attention to discolored areas, damp spots, and tears on the uniform; areas around the neck, wrists, and ears; and bandages, tourniquets, and splints. Remove contaminated spots by using an SDK or a 0.5% chlorine solution or, if possible, by cutting away the contaminated area. Always dip the scissors in a 5%chlorine solution after each cut. Recheck the area with the detection equipment. If significant contamination is found on the BDU, then remove it and spot decon the skin. To remove the BDU, follow the procedures for removing the overgarment as described in steps 4-2 through 4-4. Do not remove the patient's identification tags.

Step 6—Decon the Patient's Skin

6-1. Spot-decon. Use an SDK or a 0.5% chlorine solution to spot-decon the skin and areas of potential contamination, to include areas around the neck, wrists, and lower parts of the face. Decon the patient's identification tags and chain, if necessary.

6-2. Have the patient hold his breath, close his eyes, and lift, or assist him with lifting, his mask at the chin. Wipe his face and exposed areas of the skin with an SDK or a 0.5% chlorine solution. Starting at the top of the ear and quickly wiping downward, wipe all folds in the skin, ear lobes, upper lip, chin, dimples, and nose. Continue up the other side of the face to the top of the other ear. Wipe the inside of the mask where it touches the face. Have the patient reseal and check his mask.

CAUTION
Keep the decon solution out of the patient's eyes.

6-3. Combat medic care. The combat medic gently cuts away the bandage. He decontaminates the area around the wound and irrigates it with a 0.5% chlorine solution. If bleeding begins, he replaces the bandage with a clean one. He replaces the old tourniquet by placing a new one ½ to 1 inch above the old one. He then removes the old tourniquet and decontaminates the patient's skin with an SDK or a 0.5% chlorine solution. He does not remove a splint. He decontaminates the splint by thoroughly rinsing it, to include the padding and cravats, with a 0.5% chlorine solution.

6-4. Contaminated-waste disposal. Dispose of contaminated bandages and coverings by placing them in a contaminated-waste bag. Seal the bag and place it in the contaminated-waste dump.

Step 7—Proceed through Shuffle Pit to the Clean Treatment Area

7-1. Have the decontaminated patient proceed through the shuffle pit to the clean treatment area. To ensure that the patient's boots are well decontaminated, have him stir the contents of the shuffle pit with his boots as he crosses it. The patient's combat boots and protective mask will be removed at the entrance of the CPS or clean treatment area.

DECONTAMINANTS

Decontaminating Solution Number 2—DS2

DS2 is effective against all known toxic chemical and biological agents (except bacterial spores) if sufficient contact time is allowed. It must remain in contact with contaminated surfaces for about 30 minutes. It must be rinsed off with water. Recheck the item for contamination. DS2 can be used at temperatures above -15°F. It can be used with the M11 or M13 DAP or can be applied with brooms and swabs. It is most effective when the application is accompanied by scrubbing action.

DS2 is extremely irritating to the eyes and skin. Protective mask and rubber gloves must be worn. If DS2 contacts skin, wash area with water. Do not inhale vapors. It will cause a green or black color change upon contact with M8 detector paper and cause a false/positive reading with M9 detector paper. It will ignite spontaneously on contact with STB or HTH. It should not be spilled on the chemical protective overgarment. DS2 is a combustible liquid with a flash point of 160°F. Do not confuse it with a fire extinguisher. Spraying DS2 on surfaces above 168°F will ignite it. Iit must not be used on individual mask (damages Mylar diaphragm in voicemitter assembly). It will corrode aluminum, cadmium, tin, and zinc; it will soften leather. It may soften, remove, or discolor paint. Rinse well after use and oil metal surfaces. It is ineffective against bacterial spores.

Mixing is not required. It is issued in ready-to-use solutions consisting of the following:

Diethylenetriamine	(70%)
Ethylene Glycol Monomethyl Ether	(28%)
Sodium Hydroxide	(2%)

Super Tropical Bleach - STB

It is effective against lewisite, V and G agents, and biological agents. It must remain in contact with contaminated surface for at least 30 minutes; then, wash off with clear water. It does not effectively decon mustard agent if it has solidified at low temperatures. STB should be applied several times to porous surfaces.

It will ignite spontaneously on contact with liquid blister agent or DS2. It will give off toxic vapors on contact with G agent. It is not recommended for use on ships. Store on top deck only. It is corrosive to most metals and damaging to most fabrics (rinse thoroughly and oil metal surfaces). Should not be inhaled or allowed to touch the skin. When preparing a slurry, wear a protective mask or respiratory protective device. Should be stored in an unheated warehouse away from combustibles and metals subject to corrosion.

To make a slurry paste, mix one 50-pound drum of STB with six gallons of water. Slurry paste consists of about equal parts (by weight) of STB and water. For a dry mix, mix two shovels of STB to three shovels of earth or inert material (ashes). For a slurry mix for chemical agent contamination, mix will consist of 40 parts of STB to 60 parts of water (by weight). To mix in the M12A1 PDDA, use 1,300 pounds of STB, 225 gallons of water, 12½ pounds of antiset, and 24 ounces of antifoam.

Mask Sanitizing Solution

Use on a previously cleaned mask with filter elements/canisters removed. Place the mask face up; attach the canteen to the mask at the drinking tube. Drain one canteen full of sanitizing solution through the mask. Rinse the mask with two canteens of clear water. Immerse the mask and outserts in the sanitizing solution. Agitate the mask for five minutes. Rinse it twice in clear water, agitating two to three minutes each time. Dry all parts of the mask and reassemble. Use one gallon of solution for every 10 masks.

Fill a standard plastic canteen to the shoulder with water. Add a 0.5-gram tube of calcium hypochlorite from the water purification kit. Cover the canteen and shake vigorously for 30 seconds. Mix bulk quantities as follows: add 2.0 grams of calcium hypochlorite to 1 gallon of water. Use a ratio of about one pound of soap per gallon of water for smaller amounts of solution. Mix 2 pints of detergent to 450 gallons of water in the M12A1 PDDA.

Soaps and Detergents

Scrub or wipe the contaminated surface with a hot, soapy water solution or immerse the item in the solution.

Soaps and detergents are effective in physically removing contamination. However, casualty-producing levels of contamination may remain in the runoff water and must be considered contaminated.

Mix 75 pounds of powdered soap in 350 gallons of water. If powdered soap is not available, use bar laundry soap (75 pounds of soap cut into one-inch pieces and dissolved in 350 gallons of hot water). Use a ratio of about 1 pound of soap per gallon of water for smaller amounts of soap solution. Mix two pints of detergent to 450 gallons of water in an M12A1 PDDA.

Ammonia or Ammonium Hydroxide (household ammonia)

Is effective against G agents. Is slower-acting than sodium hydroxide or potassium hydroxide. May require the use of a Self-Contained Breathing Apparatus or special purpose mask. Ammonium hydroxide is a water solution of ammonia. No further mixing is required.

Potassium Hydroxide (caustic potash)

The same as for sodium hydroxide.

Sodium Hydroxide (caustic soda or lye)

Is effective against G agents, lewisite, and all biological agents, including bacterial spores. Will neutralize G agents on contact. Should be allowed to remain in contact with the chemically contaminated surface for about 15 minutes.

Decontaminant will damage the skin, eyes, and clothes and can cause upper respiratory or lung damage if inhaled. Full rubber protective clothing, gloves, boots, and mask are required when using. Affected area must be washed immediately with large amounts of water and flushed with diluted acetic acid or vinegar. Remove affected clothing. If eyes are involved, flush them at once with large amounts of warm water and seek medical attention. Runoff from decon operations is highly corrosive and toxic. Drain runoff into a sump and bury. Equipment must be flushed with large amounts of clear water. Is not recommended for ship use. Store on top deck only. It is corrosive to most metals. Is not recommended if less toxic caustic decontaminants are available. Will cause a red color change upon contact with M8 detector paper. Decontaminant's effectiveness is directly proportional to the strength of the solution.

Small amount—10 pounds of lye to 12 gallons of water (10% solution). Mix in an iron or steel container (never aluminum, zinc, or tin). Add lye to the water to prevent boiling and splattering due to heat being emitted. Do not handle mixing container with bare hands. Large amount (PDDE use)—prepare a solution of 227 grams (½ pound) of lye for each gallon of water. Pump 350 gallons of water into the tank unit. Connect the tank unit, pump unit, and heater together. Heat the water to 122°F. Disconnect the heater unit and add 175 pounds of lye to the heated water. Circulate the solution with the pump unit until all the lye is dissolved. The temperature will increase noticeably. Use while hot. Simultaneous mixing and applying: sprinkle dry lye on the contaminated area and then dissolve it with a spray of steam or hot water. Do not wash the lye off the surface while applying the steam or hot water. Paint removal: 1 pound of lye per 2½ gallons of water is capable of removing an average coat of paint from about 11 square yards of surface. This solution is effective in removing paint on which chemical contamination has absorbed. (Can substitute calcium hydroxide, potassium hydroxide, or trisodium phosphate for sodium hydroxide.)

Sodium Carbonate (soda ash)

Is effective against G agents and chloroacetophenone (CN). Will react rapidly with G agents, normally within five minutes. Is the preferred decontaminant for ship use. The recommended concentration is 5% by weight. There is no storage problem. Should be used with a hot solution to decon CN effectively.

Should not be used for VX. It cannot detoxify VX and creates extremely toxic by-products. Does not dissolve mustard agents or detoxify them.

Mix 10 pounds of washing soda to 12 gallons of water (10% solution).

Calcium Hypochlorite (high-test hypochlorite [HTH])

Is effective against mustards, lewisite, V agents, and all biological agents, including bacterial spores. Will react rapidly (within 5 minutes) with mustards and lewisite. Should be allowed a 15-minute contact time for biological agents. Will act faster than STB. Can be used as a dry mix or slurry.

Precautions are the same as for STB. Pure calcium hypochlorite will burn on contact with VX, HD, or DS2. Agent is more corrosive than STB. Will destroy clothing, has a toxic vapor, and will burn the skin. Protective mask and rubber gloves are the minimum protective equipment needed when handling.

Chemical: mix five pounds of decontaminant to six gallons of water (10% solution). PDDE: mix a slurry of one part decontaminant to two parts water (any heavier slurry will clog the decon apparatus). HTH should be used only if STB is not available.

Sodium Hypochlorite Solution (household bleach)

Is effective against blister and V agents and all biological agents. Will react rapidly (within 5 minutes) with blister and V agents. Should be allowed a 10- to 15-minute contact time for biological agents. Should be applied undiluted with brooms, brushes, or swabs. Is the preferred decon for ship use. A 5:1 concentration is recommended. Has a limited storage problem.

Is harmful to the skin and clothing if undiluted. Remove from the skin and clothing by flushing with water. Is corrosive to metals unless rinsed, dried, and lubricated after decon. Should be stored in a cool place.

For chemical decon, no mixing is required. For decon of cotton clothing and utensils, dilute two cups of bleach to one gallon of water. For application, dilute half and half with water and spray from the PDDE.

Dichloramine–B and Dichloramine–T

Is effective against mustard agents. May require the use of a protective mask and rubber gloves when used. Is corrosive to metal. Is not soluble in water but is soluble in certain organic solvents. Is normally mixed as a 10% solution in dichloroethane.

Diethyl Ether

Freezing point is -241°F; boiling point is 93°F. Good decontaminant for use in arctic regions. Available through medical supply facilities. Scrubbing increases its effectiveness.

Is the same as for 2-propanone.

Ethylene Glycol

Scrub on contaminated surfaces and rinse thoroughly. Removes contamination but does not neutralize it. Therefore, runoff residue must be considered contaminated. Mix equal amounts of solution and water.

Hexachloramelamine

Is effective against mustard agents. May require the use of a protective mask and rubber gloves when used. Is corrosive to metal. Is not soluble in water but is soluble in organic solvents such as gasoline, kerosene, and paint thinner.

Perchloroethylene (tetrachloroethylene)

Freezing point is -8°F; boiling point is 250°F. Is good for use in arctic climates. Is a nonflammable, synthetic solvent widely used in dry cleaning plants. Dissolves H and V agents but not G. Has a low toxicity. Scrubbing increases its effectiveness.

Physically dissolves and removes contamination but does not neutralize it.

2-Propanone (acetone)

Chemical freezing point is -203°F; boiling point is 133°F (evaporates rapidly). Good decontaminant for use in arctic regions. Commonly obtained as fingernail polish remover or paint thinners. Scrubbing increases its effectiveness.

Is extremely flammable. Does not neutralize agents. Is effective for dissolving and flushing agent by physically removing it.

Organic Solvents (gasoline, JP-4, diesel fuel, kerosene, and similar solvents)

Scrub on contaminated surfaces and rinse thoroughly.

Is the same as for ethylene glycol. May damage materials such as rubber and plastic.

Nonmilitary Decontaminating Solutions

Solution "A" contains 5% sodium bicarbonate and 5% trisodium phosphate and is used for inorganic acids, acidic caustic wastes, solvents and organic compounds, plastic wastes, polychlorinated biphenyls (PCBs), and biologic contamination.

Solution "B" is a concentrated solution of sodium hypochlorite. A 10% solution is used for radioactive materials, pesticides, chlorinated phenols, dioxin, PCBs, cyanide, ammonia, inorganic wastes, organic wastes, and biologic contamination.

Solution "C" is a rinse solution of 5% trisodium phosphate. It is used for solvents and organic compounds, PCBs and polybrominated biphenyls (PBBs), and oily wastes not suspected to be contaminated with pesticides.

Solution "D" is dilute hydrochloric acid. It is used for inorganic bases, alkalis, and alkali caustic wastes.

Patient Decon—Chlorine Solution Preparation

To decon a patient, use an SDK; however, if an SDK is not available, use a chlorine solution. If the chlorine solution is used, two concentrations of it are required. A 5% chlorine solution is required to decon gloves, aprons, litters, scissors, patient's hood, and other nonskin contact areas. A 0.5% chlorine solution is required to decon the patient's mask, skin, and splints and to irrigate his wounds. To prepare the solutions, use calcium hypochlorite granules or sodium hypochlorite (household bleach) (see Table 4.4).

Table 4.4
Preparation of Chlorine Solution for Patient Decon

HTH Ounces [3]	HTH Spoonfuls [1]	Household Bleach	Solution Percentage in 5 Gallons of Water
6	5	2 quarts	0.5
48	40	Note 2	5

Notes:

1. These measurements are used when bulk HTH is used. To measure this preparation, use the plastic spoon supplied with your meal, ready-to-eat. Use a heaping spoonful of chlorine (all that the spoon will hold). Do not shake any granules off the spoon before adding to the water.
2. Do not dilute in water because household bleach is about a 5% solution.
3. HTH is supplied in a six-ounce jar in the chemical agent patient's treatment and decon medical equipment set.

NOTES

1. Noll, G.G. and Hildebrand, M.S., *Hazardous Materials: Managing the Incident.* (Oklahoma: International Fire Service Training Association, 1994).
2. Chemical Casualty Care Office, *Medical Management of Chemical Casualties Handbook* (US Army Medical Research Institute of Chemical Defense, 1995).

5

Detection/ Decontamination/ Protection Equipment

CHEMICAL DETECTION EQUIPMENT

See Table 5.1 for comparisons of the different chemical Agent detection systems currently available.

Table 5.1
Chemical Agent Detection Systems

Equipment	Phase	Agent	Sensitivity	Time[1]
M-8 Detector Paper	Liquid only	G, VX H	100-μ drops 100-μ drops	<=30 sec
M-9 Detector Paper	Liquid only	G, VX H	100-μ drops 100-μ drops	<=20 sec
M-18A2 Detector Kit	Liquid, vapor, aerosol	GB, VX H, HN, HD, HT L, ED, MD CG AC	0.1 mg/m^3 0.5 mg/m^3 10.0 mg/m^3 12.0 mg/m^3 8.0 mg/m^3	2-3 min
M-256A1 Detector Kit	Vapor or liquid	G VX HD L CX AC, CK	0.005 mg/m^3 0.02 mg/m^3 2.0 mg/m^3 9.0 mg/m^3 3.0 mg/m^3 8.0 mg/m^3	15 min Series is longer AC--25 min

Equipment	Phase	Agent	Sensitivity	Time[1]
M-272 Water Test Kit	Water	G, VX HD, L AC	0.02 mg/m^3 2.0 mg/m^3 20.0 mg/m^3	7 min 7 min 6 min
ICAD Miniature Chemical Agent Detector		G HD L AC, CK CG	0.2-0.5 mg/m^3 10 mg/m^3 10 mg/m^3 50 mg/m^3 25 mg/m^3	2 min (30 sec for high conc) 2 min 15 sec
Field Mini-CAMS		G, V H L	<0.0001 mg/m^3 <0.003 mg/m^3 <0.003 mg/m^3	<5 min <5 min <5 min
SAW Mini-CAD	Vapor	GB GD HD	1.0 mg/m^3 0.12 mg/m^3 0.6 mg/m^3	1 min 1 min 1 min
CAM Chemical Agent Monitor	Vapor only	GA, GB, VX HD, HN	0.03 mg/m^3 0.1 mg/m^3	30 sec <=1 min
ICAM Improved Chemical Agent Monitor		G, V HD	0.03 mg/m^3 0.1 mg/m^3	10 sec 10 sec
M-8A1 Alarm Automatic Chemical Agent Alarm	Vapor only	GA, GB, GD VX HD	0.2 mg/m^3 0.4 mg/m^3 10 mg/m^3	<=2 min <=2 min <=2 min
M-90 D1A Chemical Agent Detector	Vapor only	G, V Mustard L	0.02 mg/m^3 0.2 mg/m^3 0.8 mg/m^3	10 sec 10 sec 80 sec
M-21 - RSCAAL	Vapor	G H L	90 mg/m^3 2,300 mg/m^3 500 mg/m^3	
M22 - ACADA	Vapor	G HD L	0.1 mg/m^3 2 mg/m^3 ----------	30 sec 30 sec --

Notes:
1. Time is the detection time it takes for the equipment to detect the chemical agent.

M8 Chemical Agent Detection Paper

M8 paper is a dye-impregnated paper that changes color when exposed to liquid chemical agents or aerosols. These papers cannot detect chemical agents in vapor form. M8 paper comes in 4" by 2 1/2" booklets. Each booklet contains 25 sheets of detector paper that are capable of detecting G series nerve agents (sarin, tabun, soman, and cyclosarin), V-type nerve agents, and H (mustard)-type blister agents. M8 paper can identify agents through distinctive color changes from its original off-white color: yellow-orange for G, blue-green for V, and red for H. M8 paper is typically used to identify unknown liquid droplets during chemical reconnaissance/surveillance missions. See Figure 5.1.

Figure 5.1
M8 Chemical Agent Detection Paper

M9 Chemical Agent Detector Paper

M9 paper is also a dye-impregnated paper that changes color when exposed to liquid chemical agents or aerosols. M9 detector paper is rolled into 2-inch wide by 30-feet long rolls. Although M9 paper cannot distinguish the identity of G and V nerve agents, H blister agents, and L agents, it does turn pink, red-brown, red-purple, or another shade of red when exposed to liquid or aerosol chemical, nerve, and blister agents. M9 paper is typically placed on the Battle Dress Overgarment (BDO), equipment, and vehicle exteriors to warn personnel of the presence of a liquid chemical agent. See Figure 5.2.

Figure 5.2
M9 Chemical Agent Detection Paper

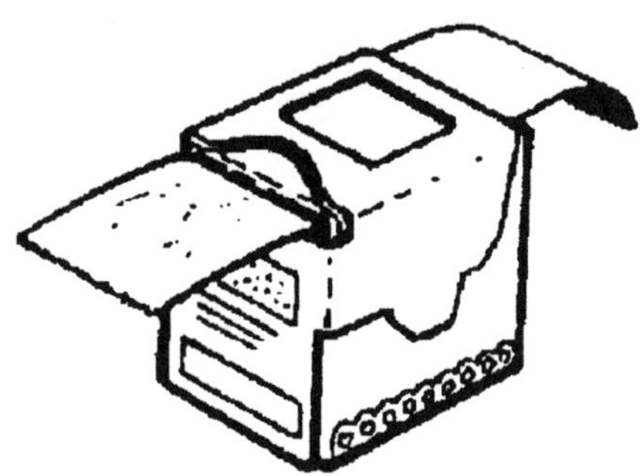

M18A2 Chemical Agent Detector Kit

The M18A2 can detect and identify dangerous concentrations of nerve agents (sarin, tabun, soman, GF and VX), blister agents (mustards, phosgene oxime, mustard-lewisite mixture, phenyl dichlorarsine [PD], ethyl dichlorarsine [ED], and methyl dichlorarsine [MD]), blood agents (hydrogen cyanide and cyanogen chloride), and choking agents (phosgene) in about one to four minutes. The kit is also used to confirm results of the M256A1 kit. The M18A2 kit contains a squeeze bulb and enough detector tubes, detector tickets, and chemical reagents needed to conduct 25 tests for each agent vapor. The kit also contains a booklet of M8 chemical agent detector paper to detect liquid agents. Agent vapor detection is indicated by the production of a specific color change in the detector tubes. The M18A2 kit is used only by special teams such as surety teams or technical escort personnel.

M256A1 Chemical Agent Detector Kit

The M256A1 kit can detect and identify field concentrations of nerve agents (sarin, tabun, soman, GF, and VX), blister agents (mustard, phosgene oxime, mustard-lewisite, and lewisite), and blood agents (hydrogen cyanide and cyanogen chloride) in both vapor and liquid forms in about 15–20 minutes.

Figure 5.3
M256A1 Chemical Agent Detector Kit

The kit consists of a carrying case containing 12 chemistry sets individually sealed in a plastic laminated foil envelope, a book of M8 chemical agent detector paper, and a set of instructions. Each detector ticket has pretreated test spots and glass ampoules containing chemical reagents. In use, the glass ampoules are crushed to release a reagent, which runs down preformed channels to the appropriate test spots. The presence of chemical agents is indicated through specific color changes on the test spots. The kit may be used to determine when it is safe to unmask, to locate and identify chemical hazards (reconnaissance), and to monitor decontamination effectiveness. See Figure 5.3.

M272 Water Test Kit

The M272 kit can detect and identify hazardous levels of nerve, blister, and blood agents in treated or untreated water resources in about 20 minutes. The kit contains enough detector tubes, detector tickets, a test bottle, and prepacked, premeasured test reagents to conduct 25 tests for each agent. The kit also contains simulants used for training.

Figure 5.4
M272 Water Test Kit

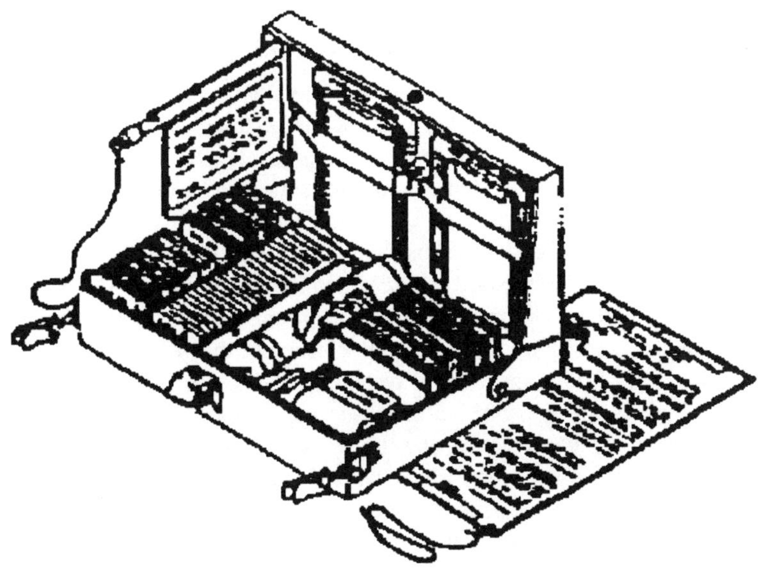

Agent detection in water is indicated by the production of a specific color change in the detector tubes or in the ticket. The M272 was fielded in 1984 and does not meet current lower-level detection requirements. See Figure 5.4.

Individual Chemical Agent Detector (ICAD)

The ICAD is a miniature lightweight chemical agent detector that can be worn by an individual. It detects G series nerve agents (GA, GB and GD), blood agents (hydrogen cyanide and cyanogen chloride), choking agents (phosgene), and blister agents (lewisite and sulfur mustard). The ICAD is about the size of an identification badge and, like a badge, it can worn on the outside of protective clothing or can be used as a point detector. It can be connected to a radio for remote operations and can be mounted on vehicles.

Miniature Continuous Air Monitoring System (Mini-CAMS)

The Mini-CAMS is a flexible, expandable system developed specifically for the detection of all common chemical warfare agents, simulants, and related compounds. The Mini-CAMS is an automated continuous air-monitoring system using gas chromatography to monitor for the presence of chemical warfare agents, simulants, and related compounds over a wide range of concentrations. The Mini-CAMS can be configured in three modes: field, fixed site, and laboratory. The field Mini-CAMS is the most appropriate configuration for emergency response.

Surface Acoustical Wave Miniature CAD (SAW Mini-CAD)

The SAW Mini-CAD is a commercially available, pocket-size instrument that can automatically monitor for trace levels of toxic vapors of both sulfur mustard and the G nerve agents with a high degree of specificity. The instrument is equipped with a vapor-sampling pump and a thermal concentrator to provide enriched vapor sample concentration to a pair of high-sensitivity, coated SAW microsensors. All subsystems are designed to consume minimal amounts of power from onboard batteries. Optimal use of the SAW Mini-CAD requires that a suitable compromise be made among the conflicting demands of response time, sensitivity, and power consumption. Maximum protection requires high sensitivity and a rapid response. The SAW Mini-CAD is able to achieve a high sensitivity with an increased vapor sampling time. However, a faster response can be achieved at a lower sensitivity setting. Testing of the SAW Mini-CAD has been performed with chemical warfare agents GD, GA, and HD. These tests were performed at a variety of concentrations and humidity levels. There were no significant effects noted due to the changes in the humidity levels for any of the chemical agents tested.

Chemical Agent Monitor (CAM) and Improved CAM (ICAM)

The CAM is a handheld instrument capable of detecting, identifying, and providing relative vapor hazard readouts for G- and V-type nerve agents and H-type blister agents. The CAM uses ion mobility spectroscopy (IMS) to detect and identify agents within one minute of agent exposure. A weak radioactive source ionizes air drawn into the system, and the CAM then measures the speed of the ions' movement. Agent identification is based on characteristic ion mobility and relative concentrations based on the number of ions detected. The ICAM has the same chemical agent detection capability as the CAM; improvements are that it is 300% more reliable and starts up 10 times faster, and the modular design is much less expensive to repair. The ICAM has the additional features of an RS-232 data communications interface and the ability to be programmed for new/different threat agents. The four-pound, 15"-long ICAM can be powered either by an internal battery or by an external source through the ICAM's combination power/fault diagnosis/RS-232 plug.

Figure 5.5
Chemical Agent Monitor

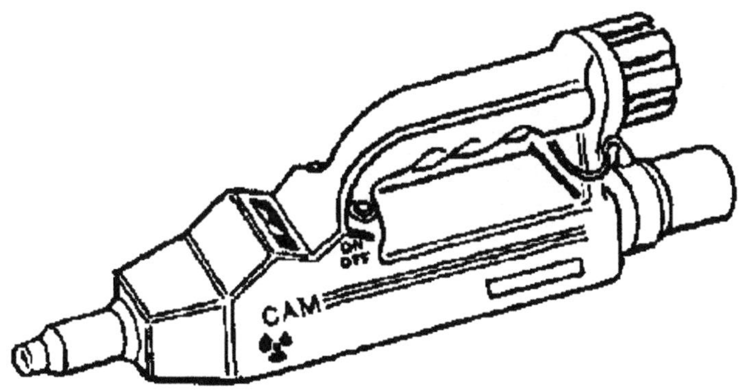

The ICAM may be used for a variety of missions, including area reconnaissance and area surveillance, monitoring of decontamination operations, and medical triage operations. The ICAM significantly reduces the level and frequency of maintenance compared to CAM without affecting performance. The ICAM sieve pack has double the capacity of the two CAM sieve packs, which results in twice the operational life of the ICAM over the CAM. When fielded, the ICAM will significantly reduce operating and sustainment costs associated with the CAM. See Figure 5.5.

M8A1 Automatic Chemical Agent Alarm (ACAA)

The M8A1 ACAA is a system that continuously samples the air to detect the presence of dangerous concentrations of G- and V-type nerve agent vapors. This system is being phased out of the inventory and will be replaced by the M22 ACADA. The M8A1 ACAA may be employed in a number of configurations, but all configurations are built around the M43A1 detector unit and the M42 alarm unit. The configurations differ primarily in their mountings and power supplies: ground-mounted and battery-operated or mounted on a vehicle and powered by the vehicle's electrical system. The M43A1 detector unit measures 6 1/2" x 5 1/2" x 11" with the battery used in ground-mounted operations adding another 7 3/4" in height.

Figure 5.6
M43 Detector Unit and M42 Alarm Unit

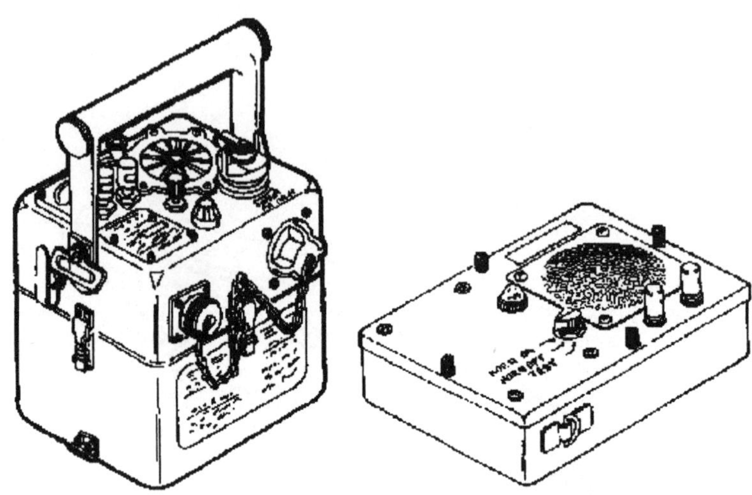

The M43A1 detector unit uses a radioisotope to ionize molecules in air that is pumped through the system and then detects electrical current changes that occur in the presence of nerve agents. The M43A1 detector unit will alarm within about one to two minutes from exposure to agent. The M42 alarm unit is a remote visual and audible alarm that measures 7" x 4" x 2 1/3". The M42 alarm unit may be placed up to 400 meters from the M43A1 detector unit to give users warning of an approaching agent cloud. See Figure 5.6.

M-90 Chemical Agent Detector (CAD)

The CAD is an automatic nerve and mustard agent detector that detects agents in vapor form. This system is currently in use by the air force. It transmits an alarm by radio to a central alarm unit.

Automatic Liquid Agent Detector (ALAD)

The ALAD is a liquid agent detector that can detect droplets of GD, VX, HD, and L as well as thickened agents. It transmits its alarm by field wire to a central alarm unit. Although the remote transmission is useful, the device detects droplets only of liquid agents. It must be used in conjunction with other point or standoff vapor agent detectors to afford a complete detection capability.

XM21 Remote Sensing Chemical Agent Alarm (RSCAAL)

The XM21 RSCAAL is an automatic scanning, passive, infrared sensor that detects nerve (GA, GB, and GD) and blister (H and L) agent vapor clouds based on changes on the infrared spectrum. It is effective at line-of-sight distances of up to five kilometers. The alarm is used for surveillance and reconnaissance missions in both vehicle- and tripod-mounted modes.

M22 Automatic Chemical Agent Detection Alarm (ACADA)

ACADA is a man-portable, point-sampling alarm system that provides significant improvement over current capabilities; it detects and identifies all nerve agents, mustard, and lewisite, by class. ACADA provides concurrent nerve and blister agent detection, improved sensitivity and response time, agent identification capability, improved interference rejection, extensive built-in test, a data communications interface, and the capability to be programmed for new threat agents. It replaces the M8A1 Alarm as an automatic point detector and augments the CAM as a survey instrument. The ACADA consists of an off-the-shelf Non-Developmental Item (NDI)—the GID-3 chemical agent alarm. A shipboard version of the ACADA is being built to address the unique interferents found aboard navy ships that cause false alarms on the NDI ACADA. The shipboard version of ACADA will serve to cover the navy's emergency requirements until the Joint Chemical Agent Detector can be fielded.

AN/KAS-1A Chemical Warfare Directional Detector (CWDD)

This is a semiportable system designed to detect nerve agent vapor clouds at ranges up to five kilometers. The AN/KAS-1A must be removed from its stowage case and set up on a preinstalled pedestal for operation. A trained, diligent operator must manually aim the detector at the suspect cloud and interpret its infrared images to determine whether or not the cloud contains nerve agent vapors. The AN/KAS-1A provides a remote video display, an enhanced capability for vapor cloud analysis, and a remote relative-bearing indicator useful for avoiding the agent cloud or other surface target with a thermal signature.

M93 NBC Reconnaissance System (NBCRS) Fox System

The M93 NBC Reconnaissance System, known as the Fox, is a high-mobility armored vehicle capable of performing NBC reconnaissance on primary, secondary, and cross-country routes throughout the battlefield. The NBCRS was procured as a Non-Developmental Item and is capable of detection, warning and sampling the effects of NBC weapons and is used as a reconnaissance vehicle to locate, identify, and mark chemical and nuclear contamination on the battlefield. The M93 Fox usually accompanies the scouts or motorized reconnaissance forces when performing its NBC mission. The NBCRS has an overpressure filtration system that permits the crew to operate the system in a shirtsleeve environment that is fully protected from the effects of NBC agents and contamination. It utilizes a secure communications system to warn follow-on forces. Samples gathered are forwarded to the Theater Area Medical Laboratory for further analysis and verification. The mobility platform is a six-wheeled, all-wheel-drive, armored combat vehicle capable of cross-country operation at speeds up to 65 mph. The Fox System is fully amphibious and is capable of swimming speeds up to 6 mph. The M93 NBCRS has been fielded worldwide to the army and Marine Corps forces.

M93A1—NBC Reconnaissance System (NBCRS) Fox System

The Block I Modification M93A1 NBCRS contains an enhanced and fully integrated NBC sensor suite consisting of the M21 RSCAAL, MM1 Mobile Mass Spectrometer, CAM/ICAM, AN/VDR-2, and M22 ACADA. The NBC sensor suite has been digitally linked together with the communications and navigation subsystems by a dual-purpose central processor system known as MICAD. The MICAD processor fully automates NBC Warning and Reporting functions and provides the crew commander full situational awareness of the Fox's NBC sensors, navigation, and communications systems. The M93A1 Fox is also equipped with an advanced position navigation system that enables the system to accurately locate and report agent contamination. The NDI mobility platform is a six-wheeled, all wheel-drive, armored vehicle capable of cross-country operation at speeds up to 65 mph. The Fox System is also fully amphibious and is capable of swimming at speeds up to 6 mph. It is used as a reconnaissance vehicle to locate, identify, and mark chemical and biological agents on the battlefield. The Fox usually accompanies the scouts or motorized reconnaissance forces when performing its mission.

Improved (Chemical Agent) Point Detection System (IPDS)

The IPDS is a new shipboard point detector and alarm that replaces the existing shipboard CAPDS. IPDS uses special elongated ion mobility cells to achieve the resolution necessary to counter false alarms caused by interferent vapors. IPDS can detect nerve and blister agent vapors at low levels and automatically provide an alarm to the ship. The unit is built to survive the harsh sea environment and the extreme electromagnetic effects found on naval ships.

Chemical Agent Point Detection System (CAPDS), MK21

CAPDS is a fixed system capable of detecting nerve agents in vapor form, using a simple baffle tube ionization spectrometer. Installed in a ship's upper superstructure level, CAPDS obtains a sample of external air, ionizes airborne vapor molecules, and collects them on a charged plate after eliminating lighter molecules via the baffle structure. When a sufficient mass of ions is collected, a preset potential is achieved, and an alarm signal is generated and sent to both Damage Control Central and the bridge. The system has been installed on almost all surface ships.

Shipboard Automatic Liquid Agent Detector (SALAD)

SALAD is an exterior, liquid agent point detection and monitoring system that will detect and alarm in the presence of liquid nerve and blister agents. It consists of a detector unit that uses chemically treated paper, optical scanners, a central processing unit, and alarms (visual and audible) on the bridge and Damage Control Central.

Joint Chemical Agent Detector (JCAD)

JCAD will provide a detector or a network of detectors capable of automatically detecting, identifying, and quantifying chemical agents (nerve, blister, and blood) inside aircraft and shipboard interiors. The device must be sufficiently sensitive to warn aircrews before accumulation, over the entire mission, of levels of agent that may cause miosis or more severe effects. JCAD will also provide handheld monitoring capabilities, protecting the individual through the use of pocket-size detector and alarm.

CHEMICAL DECONTAMINATION EQUIPMENT

M258A1 Skin Decontamination Kit (SDK)

The M258A1 consists of a pocket-size plastic case containing three sets of foil-packaged decontaminating wipes. The decontaminating sets consist of PACKET 1, containing an aqueous decon solution-soaked gauze pad, and

PACKET 2, containing a decon solution-filled glass ampoule within a gauze pad. Personnel use the two wipes successively to remove and neutralize liquid chemical agents from their skin, clothing, personal equipment, and weapons. The M258A1 is being replaced by the M291 skin decon kit. See Figure 5.7.

Figure 5.7
M258A1 Skin Decontamination Kit

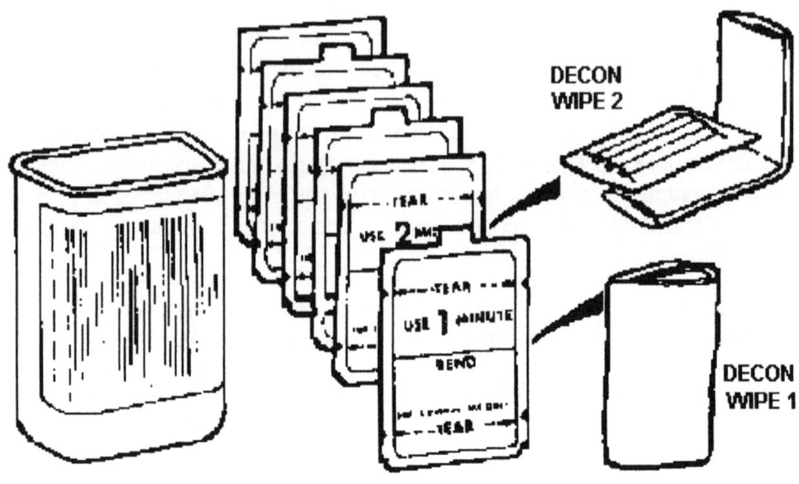

M291 Skin Decontamination Kit (SDK)

The M291 consists of a wallet like, flexible carrying pouch containing six individually sealed foil packets. Each packet contains a folded, nonwoven fiber applicator pad with an attached strap handle on one side. The pad contains a reactive and absorptive resin polymer mixture. The kit enables war fighters to remove, neutralize, and destroy chemical and biological warfare agents on contaminated skin. The kit is carried in a pocket of the Battle Dress Overgarment (BDO). See Figure 5.8.

Figure 5.8
M291 Skin Decontamination Kit

M295 Individual Equipment Decontamination Kit (IEDK)

The M295 consists of a pouch containing four individual wipe-down mitts, each enclosed in a soft, protective packet. The pouch assembly is designed to fit comfortably within the pocket of a BDO. Each wipe-down mitt in the kit consists of sorbent resin contained within a nonwoven polyester material and a polyethylene film backing. In use, resin from the mitt is allowed to flow freely through the nonwoven polyester pad material. Decontamination is accomplished through sorption of contamination by both the nonwoven polyester pad and the resin. The M295 enables the war fighter to perform basic decontamination to remove, neutralize, or destroy CB warfare agents and toxins on contaminated personal and load-bearing equipment.

M11 Portable Decontaminating Apparatus (PDA)

The 1-1/3 quart capacity M11 is used to spray DS2, Decontamination Solution 2, onto critical areas (e.g., frequently used parts) of vehicles and crew-served weapons. The M11 consists of a steel cylinder, a spray head assembly, and a small nitrogen cylinder (about three inches long). The refillable M11 can produce a spray 6 to 8 feet long and cover an area of about 135 square feet. The M11 is currently used on tanks and other systems where the larger M13 Decontaminating Apparatus, Portable (DAP) cannot be effectively stowed.

M13 Decontaminating Apparatus, Portable (DAP)

The man portable M13 consists of a vehicle mounting bracket, a prefilled fluid container, containing 14 liters of DS2 decontaminating solution, and a brush-tipped pumping handle connected to the fluid container by a hose. The fluid container and brush head are both disposable. The M13 can decontaminate 1,200 square feet per fluid container. The combination of spray pump and brush allows personnel to decontaminate hard-to-reach surfaces and remove thickened agent, mud, grease, and other material. See Figure 5.9.

Figure 5.9
M13 Portable Decontaminating Apparatus

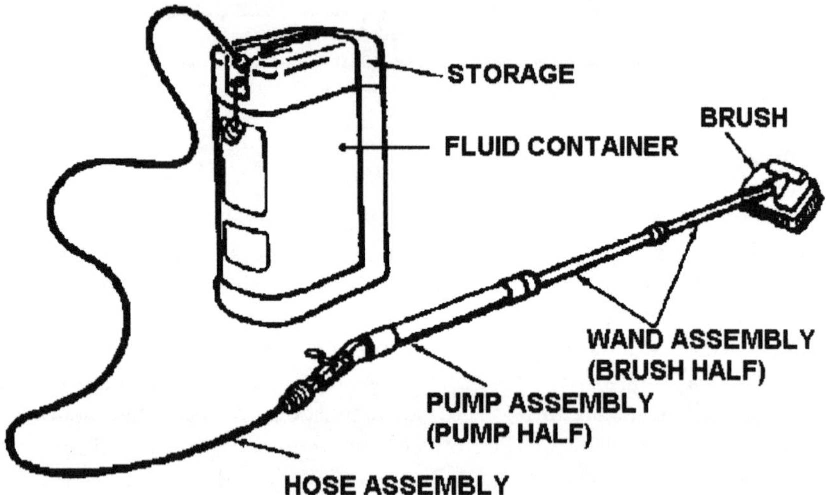

M12A1 Power-Driven Decontamination Apparatus (PDDA)

The M12A1 consists of three main components: a pump unit, a 500-gallon tank unit, and a 600-gallon-per-hour liquid fuel water heater. The M12A1 is a flexible system that can be used for purposes such as deicing, firefighting with water or foam, water pumping and transport, and personnel showering in addition to equipment and area decon. The M12A1 can pump 50 gallons of decontaminating solution per minute through both of its hoses. The integral shower assembly provides 25 shower heads. The M12A1 is typically mounted on a five-ton truck for tactical mobility but can be dismounted to facilitate air transport. The U.S. Marine Corps (USMC) has replaced the M12A1 PDDA with the M17 series Lightweight Decontamination System.

M17 Lightweight Decontamination System (LDS)

The M17 series Lightweight Decontamination System is a portable, lightweight, compact engine-driven pump and water-heating system. The system is used during decon operations. The LDS is capable of drawing water from any source and delivering it at moderate pressure and controlled temperatures. The system has an accessory kit with hoses, spray wands, and personnel shower hardware. It also includes a collapsible water bladder.

M21/M22 Modular Decontamination System (MDS)

The MDS provides the war fighter an improved capability to perform detailed equipment decontamination on the battlefield. The system replaces current methods of decontamination application (e.g., mops and brooms or the portable M13 Decontamination Apparatus), which are time-consuming and labor-intensive. The MDS improves effectiveness, reduces water usage, reduces equipment processing time, and is less labor-intensive. The MDS consists of an M21 decontaminant Pumper/Scrubber module and M22 High Pressure/Hot Water module. The M22 delivers DS2 or liquid field expedient decontaminants and is capable of drawing the decontaminant directly from a container on the ground while mounted on a trailer. The M22 provides hot water up to 3,000 psi at a rate of 5 gpm with the capability of high-volume cold water and detergent injector. It is also capable of drawing water from natural and urban water sources (such as fire hydrants) and delivering it at variable and adjustable pressures, temperatures, and flow rates. Each module (M21 or M22) may be transported or operated from a 3/4-ton trailer towed by a M1037 High-Mobility Multipurpose Wheeled Vehicle (HMMWV).

XM100 Sorbent Decontamination System

The reactive sorbent decontamination system provides a simple, rapid, and efficient system to decontaminate small and individual issue items of equipment. It is effective in all environments and presents a lowered logistics burden through improved shelf life and reduced special handling and storage needs. The system uses a catalytic component that reacts with the chemical agents being absorbed; this eliminates the potential hazard created by the off-gassing of agents from used sorbents.

INDIVIDUAL CHEMICAL PROTECTIVE EQUIPMENT

M17A2 Protective Mask

The M17A2 Protective Mask consists of a natural blend rubber facepiece; two activated charcoal filters mounted within cheek pouches; a voicemitter to facilitate communications, a drinking tube; eye-lens outserts to protect the mask's integral eye-lens and reduce cold weather fogging; an impermeable hood; and a carrier for the mask, its components, and medical items (such as the Nerve Agent Antidote Kit). The army and Marine Corps are replacing this mask with the M40 series protective masks. The navy has replaced the M17A2 protective mask with the MCU-2/P. The air force replaced it with the MCU-2A/P but retained limited quantities of extra-small M17A2s for those situations where the MCU-2A/P short is too large.

ABC-M24 Aircraft Protective Mask

This protective mask provides the wearer protection from NBC aerosols/vapors both in aircraft and on the ground. The mask consists of a wide-view, clear plastic lens embedded in a butyl rubber face blank; an integral microphone; eye-lens outserts; carrying case; antifog kit; and a hose-mounted filter canister. The mask has a microphone connection to fit the aircraft communications systems. The M24 has an adapter that allows coupling to the aircraft's oxygen supply system. The M24 is being replaced by the M45 mask.

M25A1 Tank Protective Mask

This protective mask provides the wearer protection from NBC aerosols and vapors both in the vehicle/aircraft and on the ground. The mask consists of a wide-view, clear plastic lens embedded in a butyl rubber face blank; an integral microphone; eye-lens outserts; carrying case; antifog kit; and a hose-mounted filter canister. The mask has a microphone connection to fit the armored vehicle communications systems. The M25A1 has an adapter that allows it to be coupled to the tank's filtered and temperature-controlled Gas Particulate Filtration Unit (GPFU). The M25A1 is being replaced by the M42/M42A1/M42A2 protective mask.

MCU-2A/P Protective Mask

The MCU-2A/P provides eye and respiratory protection from all chemical and biological agents as well as radioactive particulate material. The mask uses a replaceable, standard North Atlantic Treaty Organization (NATO) filter canister, which is mounted on either side of a wide-view optical-quality visor. The mask provides improved fit, comfort, and visibility relative to earlier masks and includes a drinking tube for attachment to the standard canteen and electronic voicemitter connections for improved communications.

M40/42 Series Protective Mask

The M40/42 series protective masks provide eye-respiratory face protection from tactical concentrations of Chemical and Biological (CB) warfare agents, toxins, and radioactive fallout particles. Each mask consists of a silicone rubber facepiece with an in-turned peripheral face seal and binocular rigid lens system. The facepiece is covered with a chlorobutyl second skin to provide optimum liquid agent protection for the masks. It accommodates NATO standard canisters, which can be worn on either cheek of the mask. The M40 series is designed for the individual dismounted ground warrior, while the M42 series is designed for combat vehicle crewmen. Recent improvements include a universal second skin, making the mask compatible with Joint Service Lightweight Intergrated Technology (JSLIST) and Saratoga overgarments, and ballistic/laser protective eye-lens outserts. The mask facepiece has been made a spare part, which has resulted in a significant operation and support cost savings. Use of modular parts permits the M40 series to be used in both the M40 and M42 configuration. This has resulted in significant operational and support cost savings. See Figure 5.10.

Figure 5.10
M40 and M42 Protective Mask

M43 Protective Mask

The M43 Aviator Mask consists of a form-fitting facepiece with lenses mounted close to the eyes; an integral CB hood and skull-type suspension system; an inhalation air distribution assembly for air flow regulation, lenses and hood; and a portable motor/blower filter assembly that operates on either battery or aircraft power. The M43 Type I was developed for the AH-64 aviator and is compatible with the AH-64 Integrated Helmet and Display Sight System and the Optical Relay Tube. The M43 Type II is intended for the general aviator.

M45 Aircrew Protective Mask (ACPM)

The M45 Air Crew Protective Mask is specially designed to meet the requirements of helicopter and special crews. It does not require power or forced air to provide CB protection; it provides compatibility with helicopter optical systems, aircraft displays, and night vision devices; and it has reduced weight, cost, and logistical burden when compared to the M48 mask series. The ACPM has close-fitting eye-lenses mounted in a silicone rubber facepiece with an in-turned peripheral seal and a detachable hood system and utilizes the standard NATO canister. The M45 will replace the M43 (Type II) and the M24 Aviator Mask.

M48 Protective Mask

The M48 is the third-generation M43 series masks. The M48 mask replaces the M43 Type I mask and will be the only mask for the Apache aviator for the foreseeable future. The M48 mask consists of a lightweight motor blower, a new hose assembly, a web belt, the mask carrier, facepiece carrier, eye-lens cushions, and the facepiece of the M43A1.

Aircrew Eye/Respiratory Protection (AERP)

The AERP (replaces the MBU-13/P system for aircrews) is a protective mask that enables aircrews to conduct mission operations in a chemical-biological environment. The AERP system includes a protective hood assembly with a standard MBU-12/P mask, an intercom for ground communication, and a blower assembly that provides demisting. The blower is stowed during flight operations on a bracket that is mounted inside the aircraft.

CB Respiratory System (A/P22P-14[V1, 2, 3, and 4])

The CB Respiratory System is a self-contained protective ensemble designed for all forward-deployed rotary-wing (Version 1 for U.S. Navy

[USN]) and fixed wing (Version 2-4 for USN and USMC) aircrew. The design incorporates a CB filter, dual air/oxygen supply, and a crossover manifold with ground flight selector switch to provide filtered air for hood ventilation and filtered air for oxygen for breathing. The system provides enhanced protection and offer antidrown features.

Battle Dress Overgarment (BDO)

The BDO is a camouflage-patterned (desert or woodland), two-piece, air-permeable overgarment typically worn over the duty uniform. The overgarment material consists of an outer layer of nylon cotton and an inner layer of activated charcoal-impregnated polyurethane foam.

Figure 5.11
Battle Dress Overgarment (BDO)

The BDO provides protection against chemical agent vapors and liquid droplets, biological agents (to include toxins), and radioactive alpha and beta particles. The BDO is issued in a sealed vapor-barrier bag that protects the garment from rain, moisture, and sunlight. The BDO provides 24 hours of chemical agent protection once contaminated and has a field durability of 22 days (extendable to 30 days at the discretion of field commanders). See Figure 5.11.

JSLIST Overgarment

The JSLIST Overgarment will provide 24-hour protection after 45 days of wear and six launderings. The liner currently is based upon activated carbon bead technology, replacing the bulky activated carbon foam technology in previous garments. The JSLIST Overgarment is a two-piece jacket and trouser design with an integrated hood compatible with respective service masks and second skins. It will be worn as an overgarment for the duty uniform or as a primary garment over underwear depending upon the environment and mission.

Chemical Protective (CP) Suit, OG MK-III (Navy Suit)

The Chemical Protective Overgarment (CPO) protects the wearer against all known chemical and biological agents that present a percutaneous hazard. The suit consists of a smock and separate pair of trousers. This garment will be replaced navy-wide by a superior suit developed under the auspices of JSLIST program. The Mark III chemical, biological, radiological (CBR) suit protects against chemical agent vapors, aerosols, droplets of liquid, and biological agents.

Saratoga CP Suit (USMC)

Like the BDO, the Saratoga CP Suit is an air-permeable, camouflage-patterned overgarment. Instead of carbon-impregnated foam, Saratoga uses spherical, activated carbon adsorbers immobilized in the liner fabric. This system allows for a lighter, cooler garment, which is launderable. The Saratoga provides a 24-hour protection period and has a durability of 30 days of continuous wear.

CWU-66/P Aircrew Ensemble

The CWU-66/P, a one-piece flight suit configuration, provides 24-hour protection against standard NATO threats. It is made with Von Blucher carbon spheres and is less bulky than prior ensembles. It offers a reduced thermal load burden and is compatible with aircrew life support equipment.

Chemical Protective Undergarment (CPU)

The CPU is a two-piece, lightweight undergarment made of a nonwoven fabric containing activated charcoal. When worn under the Combat Vehicle Crewmen (CVC) coverall or Battle Dress Uniform (BDU), the CPU provides 12 hours of protection and is durable for 15 days.

Joint Firefighter Integrated Response Ensemble (JFIRE)

JFIRE is a joint effort between the air force (lead agency) and the army. The JFIRE Program has developed an ensemble that will protect the military firefighters in accordance with National Fire Protection Association (NFPA) standards and provide CB protection during firefighting operations in a CB environment. JFIRE leverages the JSLIST overgarment for chemical protection, to be worn under aluminized proximity firefighting outergear and with a switchable filtered/supplied air mask with chemical warfare (CW) kit. A Commercial Off-the-Shelf (COTS) glove that can be used for both fire and CB protection will replace the need for CB gloves to be worn under standard proximity gloves. JFIRE meets several key requirements, including (1) providing 24 hours of CB agent protection against 10g/m^2 liquid agent, (2) providing firefighters CB protection in both structural and crash firefighting/rescue operation, (3) allowing firefighters to use mission-essential tools and equipment in a CB environment, (4) providing resistance to water and all standard firefighting chemicals (foam, CO_2, aircraft petroleum, oil, and lubricant), and (5) being capable of donning in eight minutes.

Suit Contamination Avoidance Liquid Protection (SCALP)

The SCALP is a four-piece suit consisting of jacket, trousers, and two footwear covers and is made from a polyethylene-coated Tyvek material. The base cloth material is of high-density polyethylene fibers, and the footwear covers have embossed polyethylene soles for durability and slip resistance. The jacket is a pullover design with an integral hood and covers the head, chest, and arms. An opening is provided for the facepiece of the individual protective mask. Two drawstrings secure the hood to the facepiece, and latex bands secure sleeves around the wrists. The trousers contain a drawstring at the waist and latex bands on the legs to secure them around the ankles. The footwear covers consist of polyethylene soles and latex bands in the upper portion to secure them to the legs. The SCALP jacket/trousers are issued separately from the SCALP footwear covers since the sizing systems are independent of one another. The SCALP, being a disposable, lightweight, impermeable suit, is worn over the BDO or CPU/duty uniform to provide additional protection from gross liquid contamination for periods up to one hour. The primary users are armor and Explosive Ordnance Disposal (EOD) personnel and personnel in collective protection who may, by necessity, be forced to leave that collective protection to perform some vital maintenance or reconnaissance function. In such situations, the SCALP will also reduce reentry time. A secondary use of the SCALP is to protect decontamination personnel from being soaked during decontamination operations. Commanders must be aware that wearing the SCALP over the BDO will place additional burden on the soldier, increasing heat stress problems already associated with wearing the BDO. The SCALP weighs approximately 1.5 pounds.

Self-Contained Toxic Environment Protective Outfit (STEPO)

STEPO provides OSHA level A protection for Army Chemical Activity/Depot, Explosive Ordnance Disposal (EOD) and Technical Escort Unit (TEU) personnel. The STEPO is a totally encapsulating ensemble for protection against chemical and biological agents, missile/rocket fuels, POL, and industrial chemicals for periods up to four hours. The ensemble incorporates two types of NIOSH-approved, self-contained breathing systems (one-hour and four-hour configurations) and a tether/emergency breathing apparatus option, a battery-powered Personal Ice Cooling System (PICS), a hands-free communications system, and standard Toxicological Agent Protective (TAP) boots and gloves. The suit is capable of being decontaminated for reuse up to five times after chemical vapor exposures. STEPO shares common, modular components with the ITAP and JFIRE ensembles, simplifying logistics and reducing costs.

Interim-Self-Contained Toxic Environment Protective Outfit (STEPO-I)

Approved as an interim system for two-hour depot operations in Immediate Danger to Life and Health (IDLH) environments, it consists of encapsulating suit made of butyl rubber-coated nylon with a polycarbonate visor. Respiratory protection is provided by one of two options—tethered clean air supply or a self-contained rebreather worn as a back-pack. Cooling is provided by an ice vest worn underneath the suit.

Improved Toxicological Agent Protective (ITAP)

ITAP replaces the M3 TAP ensemble. ITAP enhances existing capabilities by increasing personal protection and reducing the thermal burden on the wearer. ITAP also provides skin and respiratory protection during both peacetime and wartime for short-term operations in Immediately Dangerous to Life and Health (IDLH) toxic chemical environments (up to one hour), emergency life saving response, routine Chemical Activity operations, and initial entry and monitoring. ITAP shares common, modular components with the STEPO and JFIRE ensembles, simplifying logistics and reducing costs. ITAP provides splash and vapor protection against potential exposure to liquid agent when worn as a system—requirements: $10g/m^2$ HD, VX, GB, L agent challenge for one hour. It provides an optional Personal Ice Cooling System (PICS) and is functional as a system where temperatures range from 0° to 100°F when used with the cooling system. The ITAP suit and overhood are capable of being decontaminated for a minimum of five reuses, two hours per use (one hour at IDLH), after vapor and particulate contamination. After liquid contamination, ITAP suit will be decontaminated and held for disposal. The ITAP fabric is self-extinguishing, meeting NFPA 1991 standards. The fabric is also static-dissipative and does not hold a charge sufficient to set off munitions and explosives in accordance with current Explosive Safety Board requirements. The fabric is light in color to reduce operator solar heat load and is capable of being stored within the temperature range of 0° to 120°F. ITAP has a minimum shelf life of five years.

Green Vinyl Overboots/Black Vinyl Overboots (GVO/BVO)

The GVO/BVO are fitted vinyl overshoes that are worn over the combat boots to provide chemical agent protection and/or moisture vapor protection during wet weather. The impermeable GVO/BVO provide protection against chemical agents for 12 hours and are durable for up to 14 days.

Multipurpose Overboot (MULO)

The MULO is a joint-service program item under the auspices of the JSLIST program and will replace the GVO/BVO. It is made of an elastomer blend and will be produced by injection molding. It is designed for wear over the combat boot, jungle boot, and intermediate cold/wet boot. The MULO provides more durability, improved traction, resistance to POLs and flame, and better donning and doffing characteristics over standard footwear.

Chemical Protective (CP) Gloves

The CP glove set consists of a butyl-rubber outer glove for protection from chemical agents and a cotton inner glove for perspiration absorption. CP outer gloves come in three thicknesses: 7, 14, and 25 mil. The 7-mil glove is used by personnel who require a high degree of tactility, such as medical personnel and personnel engaged in electronic equipment repair. The 14-mil glove is used by personnel like aviators and mechanics, in cases when good tactility is necessary and stress to the glove is not too harsh. The 25-mil glove is used by personnel who require a durable glove to perform close combat tasks and heavy labor. The 14- and 25-mil glove sets provide protection for at least 24 hours. The 7-mil glove set should be replaced within 6 hours of exposure to a chemical agent.

COLLECTIVE CHEMICAL PROTECTIVE EQUIPMENT

M20/M20A1 Simplified Collective Protective Equipment (SCPE)

The M20/M20A1 SCPE is used to convert an interior room of an existing structure into a positive overpressure, NBC collective protection shelter where individuals can perform assigned missions without wearing the protective mask and overgarment. The system consists of a liner, protective entrance, filter canister, and support kit. The SCPE is a low-cost method of transforming a room in an existing structure into an NBC collective protection shelter for command, control, and communication (C^3), medical treatment, and soldier relief functions. M20A1 is a room liner for existing shelters.

Figure 5.12
M20/M20A1 Simplified Collective Protective Equipment

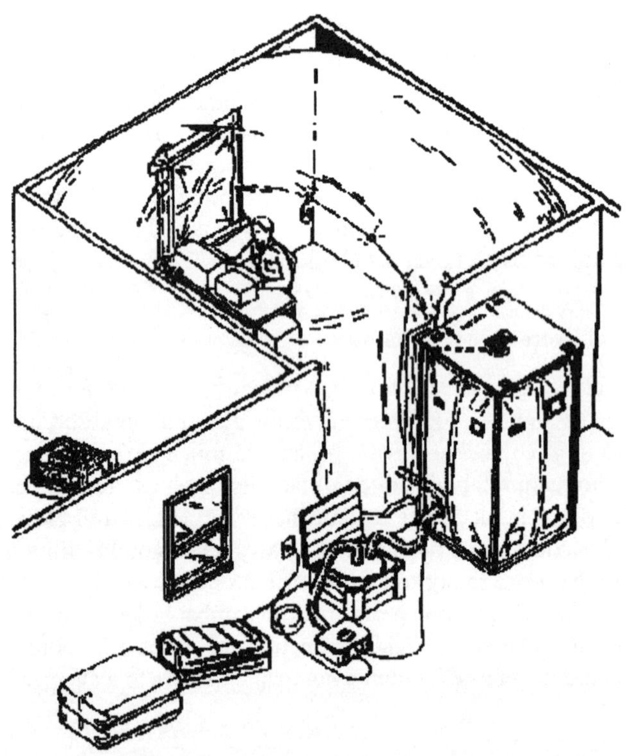

Components include a CB vapor-resistant polyethylene liner that provides a protected area in an existing structure; a collapsible, protective entrance that allows entry to/exit from the protected area; a hermetically sealed filter canister, which provides filtered air to both the liner and the protective entrance; and a support kit, which contains ducting, lighting, sealing, and repair material and an electronically powered blower. See Figure 5.12.

M28 Simplified CPE (SCPE)

The M28 SCPE is a low-cost method of transforming a room of an existing structure into an NBC collective protection shelter for command, control, and communication (C^3), medical treatment, and soldier relief functions. Components include a CB vapor-resistant polyethylene liner that provides a protected area in an existing structure; a collapsible, protective entrance that allows entry to/exit from the protected area; a hermetically sealed filter canister, which provides filtered air to both the liner and the protective entrance; and a support kit, which contains ducting, lighting, sealing and repair material and an electronically powered blower. A preplanned product improvement program to the M28 SCPE provides liquid agent resistant liners, protective liners for tents, interconnectors, and an interface with environmental control units. The improved SCPE also allows more people to enter at one time, and protects hospitals under tents.

M51 Protective Shelter, CB

The M51 shelter is a trailer-mounted system that consists of the following major components: a 10-man shelter, a protective entrance, and a support system. The shelter and protective entrance support themselves through air-filled ribs. The protective entrance minimizes carryover of vapor contamination from outside to inside the shelter and the rate of entries to the shelter to prevent loss of shelter over-pressure.

Figure 5.13
M51 Shelter System

The air-handling system is permanently mounted in the trailer and provides forced, filtered, and environmentally conditioned air to the shelter.The M51 is mostly used by battalion aid stations and other medical units. It can also be used as a temporary rest and relief shelter. Currently, the M51 utilizes outdated technologies and is being replaced with CBPS. Very few M51s remain serviceable and logistically supportable. This system can be erected and employed by 4–6 personnel in approximately one hour. This system provides heat stress relief from the effects of MOPP for 12–14 personnel. See Figure 5.13.

Chemically Protected Deployable Medical System (CP DEPMEDS)

The army's CP DEPMEDS program is a joint effort with the air force to insert environmentally controlled collective protection into currently fielded hospital shelters. The requirement is to be able to sustain medical operation for 72 hours in a chemical-contaminated environment. Environmentally controlled collective protection is provided through the integration of M28 SCPE, chemically protected air conditioners, heaters, water distribution and latrines, and alarm systems. M28 SCPE provides protection to existing tents and passageways within the hospital. DEPMEDS shelters are protected through the replacement of existing shelter seals with those that are CB-protected. The Field Deployable Environmental Control Unit provides air conditioning, and the army space heater provides heating. Both environmental control units are chemically protected through the addition of a CB kit. To sustain approximately 500 patients and staff, chemically protected latrines and water distribution systems have been developed.

CB Protective Shelter (CBPS)

CBPS is a highly mobile, rapidly deployable shelter system designed to be used for Echelon I and II forward area medical treatment facilities as a replacement for the M51. The system is self-contained and self-sustaining. The CBPS consists of a dedicated M1113 Expanded Capacity Vehicle (ECV), a Lightweight Multipurpose Shelter (LMS) mounted onto the vehicle, a 300-square-foot air beam-supported CB protected shelter, and a High Mobility Trailer with a 10kW tactical Quiet Generator Set. The ECV and LMS transports a crew of four and their gear. All medical equipment required for the shelter is transported in the LMS or on the trailer. The CB shelter is rolled and carried on the rear of the LMS during transport. The CBPS is operational within 20 minutes with a crew of four. All power required to support operations is provided by the ECV engine or with the 10kW generator for limited power. The system is environmentally conditioned by a hydraulically powered environmental support system, which provides filtered air, heating, air conditioning, and electrical power.

Portable Collective Protection System (PCPS)

The transportability and ease of use of the Portable Collective Protection System (PCPS) permit mobility and flexibility in chemically contaminated areas. PCPS can be erected by four personnel within 30 minutes wearing MOPP 4 gear. The protective shelter is divided into a main area and two smaller compartments, the entry area and the storage area. When overpressure is applied, the protective shelter provides protection from liquid and vapor chemical agents. An air lock (protective entrance) allows purging of possible chemical agent vapors and additional decontamination of personnel entering the main area.

Chemically Hardened Air Transportable Hospital (CHATH)

The air force's CHATH program is a joint effort with the army to enable medical personnel to deploy and set up in chemical and biological threat areas and operate in chemically and biologically active environments. CHATH allows personnel to perform their hospital duties in a Toxic Free Area. CHATH upgrades Air Transportable Hospitals (ATHs) retaining the same medical equipment and personnel. CHATH uses existing and modified U.S. Army equipment to line the current ATH tents providing an airtight shelter. The Human Systems Program Office developed a Chemically Hardened Air Management Plant (CHAMP). The CHAMP filters chemically and biologically contaminated air, recirculates and filters interior air to maintain a clean hospital standard, and provides heating, cooling, and overpressurization to the hospital. The CHAMP can be operated from standard electrical sources or from its own internal generator. The CHAMP comes equipped with an automatic transfer switch to maintain power after base power is shut off. The automatic transfer switch starts the diesel generator after three seconds of power interruption. The CHAMP allows the CHATH to be staged near war fighters in the field in a bare base environment. The CHATH can be deployed in increments of 10, 25, and 50 beds. This flexibility of the CHATH system helps ensure the best medical care as near the crisis area as possible.

Shipboard Collective Protection System

Shipboard CPS is an integral part of the heating, ventilating, and air-conditioning (HVAC) systems on new construction ships. CPS provides each protected zone on the ship with filtered air at an overpressure of 2.0 inches water gauge. CPS is modular and is based on a navy-improved version of the

200 cfm M56 filter. CPS includes filters, filter housings, high-pressure fans, air locks, pressure control valves, low-pressure alarm system, and personnel decontamination stations.

Selected Area Collective Protection System

Selected Area CPS (SACPS) is designed to be easily adaptable to current ships to provide selected spaces (e.g., command and control, berthing areas) with an affordable CPS system. SACPS is modular and is based on a navy-improved version of the 200 cfm M56 filter. SACPS is easily integrated into the ship's existing HVAC system and includes filters, filter housings, a high-pressure fan, an air lock, a pressure control valve, and a low-pressure alarm system.

CHEMICAL AGENT MEDICAL DEFENSE

Nerve Agent Antidote Kit Mark I (NAAK)

The NAAK Mark I contains two AtroPen autoinjectors, one containing 2 mg of atropine and the second 600 mg of pralidoxime chloride (2-PAM Cl), in a compact package that facilitates emergency use.

Figure 5.14
Nerve Agent Antidote Kit Mark I (NAAK MKI)

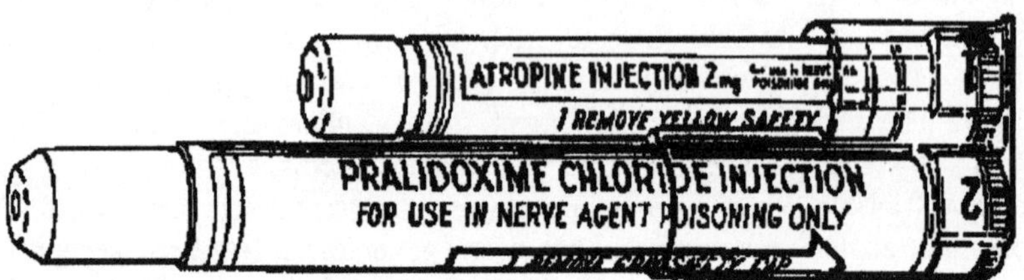

Atropine is used as a treatment for nerve agent poisoning. The other injector contains 2-Pam Chloride. These drugs are fully approved for chemical agent treatment by the Food and Drug Administration (FDA). NAAK must be stored in a controlled room temperature of 59°–86°F with limited access. The shelf life is five years. Side effects of inadvertent use of atropine includes inhibition of sweating, dilation of pupils, dry mouth, decreased secretions, mild sedation, and increased heart rate. The side effects of the inadvertent use of 2-PAM-Cl include dizziness, blurred vision, nausea, and vomiting. These effects are insignificant in a nerve agent casualty. See Figure 5.14.

Convulsant Antidote Nerve Agent (CANA) Autoinjector

Convulsant Antidote Nerve Agent (CANA) is a convulsion antidote for nerve agents. CANA is an autoinjector that contains 2 ml of diazepam (more commonly known as Valium) as the anticonvulsant. Diazepam is fully approved for this application by the FDA. It is used only as buddy-aid and never self-injected. Additionally, this item must be stored at a controlled room temperature of 59°–86°F. The shelf life is two years. See Figure 5.15.

Figure 5.15
Convulsant Antidote for Nerve Agent (CANA)

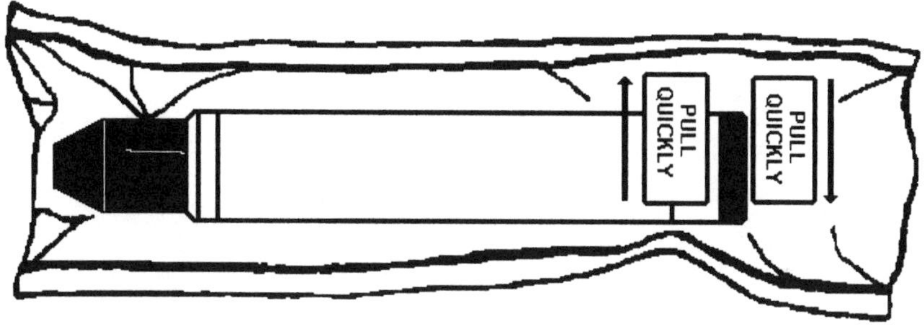

Nerve Agent Pyridostigmine Pretreatment (NAPP) Tablets

NAPP (also referred to as NAPS) contains pyridostigmine bromide tablets as a pretreatment for certain nerve agent poisoning (GA and GD). NAPP is designated as an Investigational New Drug (IND) by the FDA for this application. Pretreatment improves the efficiency of therapy for nerve agent poisoning. The drug is available as a 30 mg tablet and should be taken orally, under orders, three times a day. The standard packing is a plastic and aluminum foil blister pack containing 21 tablets. Upon orders, NAPP is taken once every eight hours. Since NAPP is still considered an Investigational New Drug, the following release procedures apply. The theater commander in chief (CINC) states the threat and need to use NAPP to the Joint Chiefs of Staff (JCS). The assistant secretary of defense for health affairs requests that the FDA allow the Deparment of Defense (DOD) to use NAPP under IND protocol and also requests a waiver of informed consent. After this approval is received, the CINC can authorize release of NAPP to the individual soldiers. NAPP must be stored under refrigeration between 35°–46°F. NAPP cannot be left out of refrigerated conditions for more than a cumulative period of 6 months. The shelf life of NAPP is five years. The side effects include increased gastrointestinal activity, increased urination, headaches, runny nose, tingling, difficulty breathing, slurred speech, and increased blood pressure.

6

Appendix: Abbreviations and Acronyms

-A-

ABC - Airway, Breathing, and Circulation
AC - Hydrogen Cyanide
ACAA - Automatic Chemical Agent Alarm
ACADA - Automatic Chemical Agent Detection Alarm
ACPM - Aircrew Protective Mask
ADS - Area Detection System
AERP - Aircrew Eye Rerspiratory Protection
ALAD - Automatic Liquid Agent Detector
AMT - Ambulatory Medical Treatment
ASTM - American Society for Testing and Materials
ATH - Air Transportable Hospital

-B-

BDO - Battle Dress Overgarment
BDU - Battle Dress Uniform
BVO - Black Vinyl Overboot
BZ - 3-Quinuclidinyl benzilate

-C-

C^3 - Command, Control, Communications
CA - Bromobenzylcyanide
CAM - Chemical Agent Monitor
CANA - Convulsant Antidote Nerve Agent
CAPDS - Chemical Agent Point Detection System
CARC - Chemical Agent Resistant Coating
CARDS - Chemical Agent Remote Detection System
CAS# - Chemical Abstracts Service #
CAWM - Chemical Agent Water Monitor
CB - Chemical and Biological (also C/B)
CBIRF - Chemical Biological Incident Response Force
CBPS - Chemical Biological Protective Shelter
CBR - Chemical Biological Radiological
CBW - Chemical and Biological Warfare
CDC - Centers for Disease Control

CESM - Chemical Environment Survivability Mask
CESS - Chemical Environment Survivability Suit
CFM - Cubic Feet per Minute
CG - Phosgene
CHAMP - Chemically Hardened Air Management Plant
CHATH - Chemically Hardened Air Transportable Hospital
CINC - Commander in Chief
CJCS - Chairman of the Joint Chief of Staff
CK - Cyanogen Chloride
CN - Chloroacetophenone
CNS - Central Nervous System
COTS - Commercial Off-the-Shelf
CP - Chemical Protective (also, collective protection)
CPE - Collective Protection Equipment
CPFC - Chemical Protective Footware Cover
CPO - Chemical Protective Overgarment
CPS - Collective Protective Shelter
CPU - Chemical Protective Undergarment
CS - *o*-Chlorobenzylidenemalononitrile
CSEPP - Chemical Stockpile Emergency Preparation Program
CVC - Combat Vehicle Crewman
CVCUS - Combat Vehicle Crewman Uniform System
CW - Chemical Warfare
CWA - Chemical Warfare Agent
CWC - Chemical Weapons Convention
CWDD - Chemical Warfare Directional Detector (AN/KAS-1A)
CWS - Chemical Warfare Service
CX - Phosgene Oxime

-D-

DA - Diphenylchloroarsine
DAP - Decontaminating Apparatus Portable
DC - Diphenylcyanoarsine
DED - Detailed Equipment Decon
DEPMEDS - Deployable Medical Systems
DM - Adamsite
DOD - Department of Defense
DP - Diphosgene
DPE - Demilitarization Protective Ensemble
DS2 - Decontamination Solution 2
DTD - Detailed Troop Decon

-E-

ECV - Expanded Capacity Vehicle
ED - Ethyl Dichlorarsine
EMS - Emergency Medical Services
EMT - Emergency Medical Technician
EOD - Explosive Ordnance Disposal
EPA - Environmental Protection Agency

-F-

F - Fahrenheit
FDA - Food and Drug Administration
FMC - Field Medical Card

-G-

GA - Tabun
GB - Sarin
GC - Gas Chromatography
GD - Soman
GF - Cyclohexyl-sarin
GPFU - Gas Particulate Filter Unit
GVO - Green Vinyl Overboot

-H-

HazMat - Hazardous Materials
HD - Distilled Sulfur Mustard
HE - High Explosive
HEPA - High Efficiency Particulate
HL - Mustard-Lewisite Mixture
HMMWV - High-Mobility Multipurpose Wheeled Vehicle
HN1 - Nitrogen Mustard 1
HN2 - Nitrogen Mustard 2
HN3 - Nitrogen Mustard 3
HSI - Hyper Spectral Imageing

HQ - Headquarters
HT - Sulfur Mustard
HTH - High Test Hypochlorite
HVAC - Heating Venting and Air-conditioning

-I-

ICAD - Individual Chemical Agent Detector
ICAM - Improved Chemical Agent Detector
ICDS - Improved Chemical Detection System
ICE - Individual Chemical Equipment
IDLH - Immediate Danger to Life and Health
IEDK - Individual Equipment Decon Kit
IG - Inspector General
IMS - Ion Mobility Spectroscopy
IND - Investigational New Drug
IPDS - Improved Point Detection System
IPE - Individual Protective Equipment
ITAP - Improved Toxicological Agent Protection

-J-

JBPDS - Joint Biological Point Detection System
JBREWS - Joint Biological Remote Early Warning System
JCAD - Joint Chemical Agent Detector
JCAHO - Joint Commission on Accreditation of Healthcare Organizations
JCBAWM - Joint Chemical Biological Agent Water Monitor
JCBUD - Joint Chemical and Biological Universal Detector
JCPE - Joint Collective Protection Equipment
JCRS - Joint Canteen Refill System
JCS - Joint Chiefs of Staff
JFIRE - Joint Firefighter Integrated Response Ensemble
JP8 - Aviation Fuel
JPACE - Joint Protective Aircrew Ensemble
JSAM - Joint Service Aviation Mask
JSGPM - Joint Service General Purpose Mask
JSLIST - Joint Service Lightweight Integrated Technology
JSLNBCRS - Joint Service Light NBC Reconnaissance System
JSLSCAD - Joint Service Lightweight Standoff Chemical Agent Detector
JSNBCRS - Joint Service NBC Reconnaissance System
JSWILD - Joint Service Warning and Identification LIDAR Detector
JTCOPS - Joint Transportable Collective Protection System
JWARN - Joint Warning and Reporting Network

-L-

L - Lewisite
LCE - Load-Carrying Equipment
LD_{50} - Median Lethal Dose
LDS - Lightweight Decontamination System
LIDAR - Light Detection And Ranging
LMS - Lightweight Multipurpose Shelter
LNBCRS - Light NBC Reconnaissance System
LSCAD - Lightweight Stand-off Chemical Agent Detector
LSCD - Laser Stand-off Chemical Detector
LSD - Lysergic

-M-

MCPE - Modular Collective Protection System
MD - Methyl Dichlorarsine
MDS - Modular Decontamination System
MICAD - Multipurpose Integrated Chemical Agent Detector
MOPP - Mission-Oriented Protective Posture

MS - Mass Spectrometry
MSHA - Mine Safety and Health Administration
MTF - Medical Treatment Facility
MULO - Multipurpose Overboot

-N-

NAADS - Nerve Agent Antidote Delivery System
NAAK - Nerve Agent Antidote Kit
NAAS - Nerve Agent Antidote System
NAPP - Nerve Agent Pyridostigmine Pretreatment
NATO - North Atlantic Treaty Organazation
NBC - Nuclear, Biological, and Chemical
NBCRS - NBC Reconnaissance System (Fox Vehicle)
NCO - Non-Commissioned Officer
NDA - New Drug Application
NDI - Non-Developmental Item
NFPA - National Fire Protection Association
NIH - National Institutes of Health
NIOSH - National Institute for Occupational Safety and Health

-O-

OG - Overgarment
OS - Operator's Spray-down
OSHA - Occupational Safety and Health Administration

-P-

PBB - Polybominatedbiphenyl
PCB - Polychlorinatedbiphenyl
PCPS - Portable Collective Protection System
PD - Phenyl Dichlorarsine
PDA - Portable Decontamination Apparatus
PDDA - Power-Driven Decontamination Apparatus
PDDE - Power-Driven Decon Equipment
PICS - Personal Ice Cooling System
PMCD - Program Manager for Chemical Demilitarization
POL - Petroleum, Oil, and Lubricant
PPE - Personal Protective Equipment
PPW - Patient Protective Wrap
PS - Chloropicrin
PSI - Pounds per Square Inch
PW - Personal Wipe-down

-R-

RSCAAL - Remote Sensing Chemical Agent Alarm

-S-

SA - Arsine
SACPS - Selected Area Collective Protection System
SALAD - Shipboard Automatic Liquid Agent Detector
Saratoga - Protective Overgarment
SAW - Surface Acoustic Wave
SCALP - Suit Contamination Avoidance Liquid Protection
SCAMP - Shipboard Chemical Agent Monitor, Portable
SCBA - Self-Contained Breathing Apparatus
SCPE - Simplified Collective Protective Equipment
SCUD - Surface-to-Surface Missile System
SD - Stand-off Detector
SD - Skin Decontamination
SDK - Skin Decontamination Kit
SDS - Sorbent Decon System
STB - Super Tropical Bleach
STEPO - Self-Contained Toxic Environment Protective Outfit
STEPO-I - Interim Self Contained Toxic Environment Protective Outfit

-T-

TAP - Toxicological Agent Protective boots and gloves
TAPES - Toxicological Agent Protective Ensemble Self-contained
TEU - Technical Escort Unit
TGD - Thickened Soman
THD - Thickened Distilled Mustard
TPU - Tank and Pump Unit

-U-

UNSCOM - United Nations Special Commission
USN - U.S. Navy
USMC - U.S. Marine Corps

-V-

VPU - Vapor Protective Undergarment
VR-55 - Soman
VX - Nerve Agent
VX - Soman

-W-

WMD - Weapons of Mass Destruction

Index

About the Author

STEVEN L. HOENIG is a forensic chemist. Educated at the Polytechnic Institute of New York and at Long Island University, he served in the New York Army National Guard as a Nuclear, Biological, and Chemical Specialist with the 42nd Chemical Company and as a NBC Reconnaissance Sergeant with the 102nd Engineer Battalion.